SEMPER FELIXES

CAT HIGH

Knowledge
Agility

Independence
Attitude

EST. MDCCCXXXVIII

Paw Prints

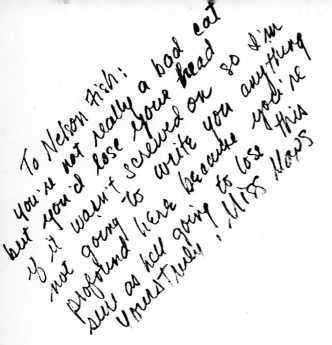

To Nelson Fish:
you're not really a bad cat
but you'd lose your head
if it wasn't screwed on so I'm
not going to write you anything
profound here because you're
sure as hell going to lose this
YoursTruly, Miss Haps

CONGDON & WEED, INC.

DEDICATION

This year *Paw Prints* is dedicated to Coach Fred Ball Whiskers. F'Ball, as we affectionately refer to him, is retiring this year, after 12 seasons, as coach of the Ratters.

Principal Grimm really summed up the magic of F. Ball Whiskers when he said in his now famous "Fourth-and-Long Speech" that "no other coach in Cat High History has been able to transform a bunch of purrsnickity, catnip-crazed carousers into a disciplined football team with the inner workings of a Swiss watch."

Indeed (and in practice), Coach F. Ball Whiskers has succeeded in building a better "Ratter" team. The record book didn't always show it, but our playbook did. Inventions like the Leaning-Tower-of-Pizza play (a twist on the Statue-of-Liberty, except the quarterback leans to one side), the bury-the-bone play (very successful against Dog High), and the Hickory-Dickory-Dock play (which had the mice of Mouse High running round the clock) all bear the Whiskers trademark. In addition, consider Coach Whisker's use of new equipment—nose plugs for the games against the skunks of Scent Vincent's and ear plugs against the roosters of Rooster Tech—have put him in a league with the Cat High Football Hall-of-Famouser Vince Lompawdri.

F.B.W. was as big an inspurration off as on the field. His spirit and his iconocatstic verve make us purroud of him. You never heard FBW tiring out old saws like 1% inspurration 99% perspiration, or the best way to win is to beat the other team! No, the washwords we have soaked up are "Win hard, play hard! *Losing Sucks.*"

When FBW says "tackle," you don't bait a hook, you grab the guys by the whatever and bring 'em down! No pussyfooting with the Coach, no sir! When he calls a pass play you don't go nuzzle your girlfriend, you put the patented Whisker grip on the seams and throw a perfect spiral down-field. FBW has taught us the meaning of hard work and the value of winning and even a locker room joke or two.

FBW, we seniors salute you with our cheers, our marching bands and our school spirit. We say "Hail to the Chief," for you have taught us much.

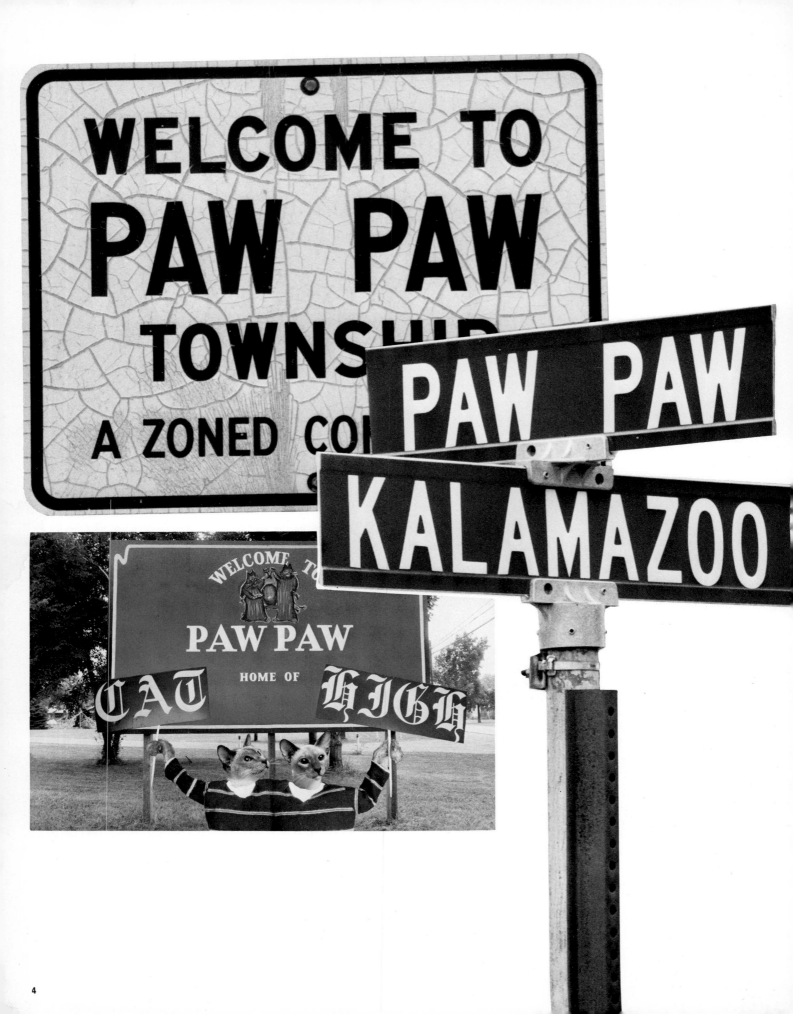

The town that is building for tomorrow, or maybe the day after.

Paw Paw is a thriving little town in the county of Cheshire. It is totally surrounded by its two neighboring communities, Minniemousapolis and St. Paw. Together the towns comprise what their residents refer to as the Tri-Kitty Area.

Famous in American history as the site of the Battle of Gerbil Hiil, Paw Paw is a short drive from Hartz Mountain, where Paw Pawians enjoy all manner of recreational activity except swimming. Within a slightly larger radius are the cultural centers of Morristown and Chatham. Many graduates of Cat High School, the town's celebrated educational institution, have gone on for post-grad work at the Chatham Vocal Arts Conservatory (motto: "Cat, Got Your Tongue?") and the Morristown School of Self-Grooming. Cat High, incidentally, has one of the highest per catpita National Meowit Scholarship rates in the county.

Until ten years ago, Paw Paw was primarily agricultural, with a work force renowned for its ability to scratch holes in the ground several times a day. Now, however, industry is being attracted to the locale, including the Puss-in-Boots shoe factory and the producers of the revolutionary new Anytime-Is-Snacktime cat-food (in a can that pussies can claw open all by themselves).

The population of Paw Paw at last Cat Census was either 19,789 cats or 6,334 (it proved very hard to get the cats to answer the doorbell when the census-taker called). The typical Paw Paw family has 5.2 children every eight months and eats 547 times its own weight in canned tuna annually.

Leisure-time activities, as in any feline community, are very big in Paw Paw. The adults like to lie around listening to classical music and the kids like rock, hot rods and wild times. Nothing, however, prevents everybody from getting a good night-and-day's sleep.

Paw Paw residents enjoy a variety of movies and plays but take special pleasure in the many fish stores, butcher shops, catessens and ratstaurants at the Paw Paw Maul. The town has its own television station, CATV, with its own rare breed of newscatters.

The citizens of Paw Paw walk their streets with tails raised high. In every way they strive to live up to the ideals of their forebears, whenever they can remember what the heck they are.

ADMINISTRATION
AND FACULTY

If Sue Purr married Fred Fur she'd be Sue Purr Fur! ♡

Dear Seniors:

It chokes me up to write this, my farewell speech, the last in a long succession of terrific speeches in my career as principal.

First, I'd like to say thanks for the Listerine—whoever you are. Second, I'd like to say congratulations for making it through these past four years. If anyone didn't think you would, it was me. As my wife Fleasia said, "If ever there was a bunch of ne'er do wells, it's got to be this senior class."

What have four years of working and learning together taught us about the feline condition? That is a question that leads to the really big questions: Is there life after Cat High? Was there life at Cat High to begin with? Is <u>one</u> in the paw really worth <u>two</u> in the bush? And, finally, why would anyone want to ruin perfectly good anchovies by putting them on a pizza?

I'd like to leave you with a thought: it has been said that success is one percent inspiration and 99 percent perspiration. On the other hand, who's ever seen a cat sweat?

Sincerely,

Thelonius T.G. Bones Grimm IX

Principal

EST. MDCCCXXXVIII

Dr. Seymour Fretmore

Superintendent of Paw Paw Public Schools

Make us purroud of you! — Fretmore

AD-MINIST-RATION

Thackery Furbanks

Cat High Vice Principal, Science Teacher
"Whatever happened at Cat High,
just remember—don't flunk your future."

Mrs. Fleasia Grimm

Principal's Wife
"Even though you're graduating this year,
you still look like the same cats
that graduated last year."

TEACHERS SAY THE DAMNDEST THINGS

"Get the point? Huh? Get the point?"

"Good citizenship— that's what it's all about."

"Stop that hissing!"

"A good mind is like a good sewing machine —it can create anything."

"Ceux qui aiment l'amour sont aimés."

"This locker room smells like a wet dog."

"I'm out to lunch—see my computer."

"The best way to win in sports is to beat the other team."

Mademoiselle Ouiounon

French, Art Teacher
"The heart has its raisins, and the raisins don't know anything about it."

Mr. Nobull

Boys Gym, History of War
"There's no excuse for excuses."

Good ~~nickname~~ luck
P. E. Nobull

Miss Hatch

Gerbil Skills, English 1,2
"Give me a cat at an impressionable age and she's mine forever."

Mr. Ratterwrong

Ancient Egyptian History, Greek
"Are you asking me or telling me?"

Miss Shugenah

Librarian
"Now where would you look that up?"

Mr. Humbert
Sex Education, Girls Basketball,
Volleyball, Field Mouse Hockey
"Your body is a tabernacle;
worship it."

Mr. Culpepper
Drivers Education, Fencing Coach
"Give the other cat the right of way."

Mr. Manx
Mewsic Appreciation, Band Director
"Don't toot 'til I raise my paw."

Miss Maps

Social Studies
"Today's film is about a society
very unlike our own."

Sister Mary Spade

Cat-Holicism and Dog-Ma
"Your task on this earth is
to prepare your soul for the afterlives."

Mr. Washington

Afro-American Studies
"This is a scream. D + ."

Miss Mouseberger
Yearbook Advisor, Home Economics
"Yes, I know you want a career, but you still have to learn how to boil an egg."

Mr. Bandersnatch

Algebra, Trigonometry, Computer Science
"Have you seen my glasses?"

Miss Cordoba

Romance Languages
"Do you want to say it your way or the right way?"

Miss Parsely

English 3,4
"The great classics have much to tell us about life right here in Paw Paw."

N — I await your first published novel. Please catbooks! A.E.P.

School Nurse
"Take care of yourselves."

THE CATS IN HATS

Judging from the line of starry-eyed tomcats always faking fleas or thorns in the paws outside of her office, we think that Nurse Hummingbird caused more heartaches than she cured stomachaches this year. Of course, that's no surprise considering our own Florence Nightingale was Cat High's Homecoming Queen just a few years ago. Besides her obvious contribution to school morale, Nurse Hummingbird also cares deeply about the health of the students, as shown by the sign she has hanging on her wall that warns: "The Sturgeon General has declared catnip taking is hazardous to your health." Medical emergencies are rare at our school, but Nurse Hummingbird acted swiftly and called an ambulance the time Melvin Lick fainted when she told him: "Take two aspurrin and claw me in the morning." In sickness and in health, we don't need a "second opinion" when we say, we'd rather be in traction with you than anybody else.

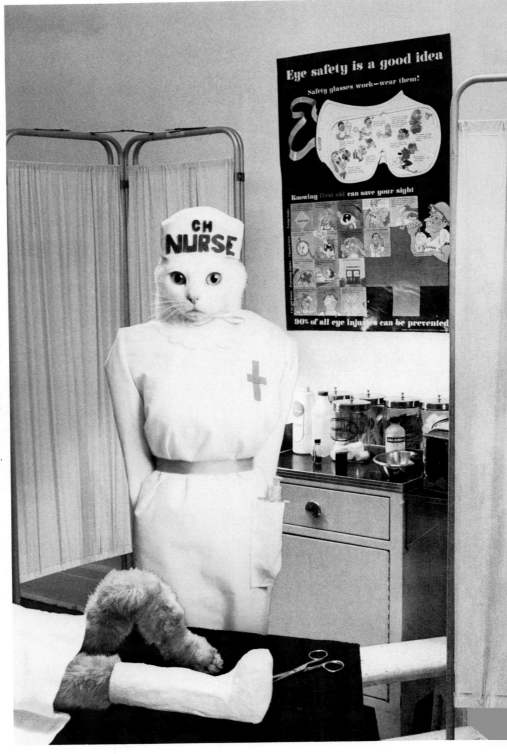

14

Kitchen Help!!!

Fine wines, the best caviar, large portions, reasonable prices: the cateteria has none of these. Nevertheless, we do have Monsieur Pierre Le Pan (straight off the boat from somewhere) and his galloping gourmet assistants Leo and Vinnie. Their tuna dogs are guaranteed to be the best this side of Tunasia. Uncork the champagne and let's toast our cats in the hats!

CENTER: Cat High Chef, Pierre Le Pan
LEFT: Preparation Technician, Leo Lukashewski
RIGHT: Food Alchemist, Vinnie Ishkibble

Mr. Joe Joe,

Sanitation Engineer

If you drop a tuna-lid on the floor,
Or write something clever on the bathroom door,
When it's not there the next day, you'll know why:
Because Joe, the Sanitation Engineer, has been by.
Thanks, Joe, for making Cat High so neat,
By keeping the hairballs off our little cat feet.

FACULTY FAVORITES

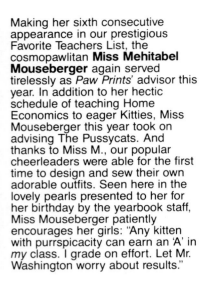

Making her sixth consecutive appearance in our prestigious Favorite Teachers List, the cosmopawlitan **Miss Mehitabel Mouseberger** again served tirelessly as *Paw Prints'* advisor this year. In addition to her hectic schedule of teaching Home Economics to eager Kitties, Miss Mouseberger this year took on advising The Pussycats. And thanks to Miss M., our popular cheerleaders were able for the first time to design and sew their own adorable outfits. Seen here in the lovely pearls presented to her for her birthday by the yearbook staff, Miss Mouseberger patiently encourages her girls: "Any kitten with purrspicacity can earn an 'A' in *my* class. I grade on effort. Let Mr. Washington worry about results."

The girls of CH were fighting over front row seats in **Thackery Furbanks'** science class this year. "He hasn't blinded me with science he's blinded me with his eyes," said Phyllis Snippitt in her Favorites questionnaire. Others concurred. He received an unprecedented twenty-five first place votes among the she-cats. Good looks, dapper dress, and cute markings catapulted him onto the Favorites list.

But Mr. Furbanks' popularity wasn't without controversy. He received twenty Least Favorite votes among the boys. As Clawford MacLeash put it, "Where's it written you have to wear a skirt to get a decent grade around here?" Controversy aside, Thackery Furbanks is going to be Principal next year, so we guess this will be his last chance to receive *this* honorary citation.

Though clearly a dark horse, **Mr. Washington** was chosen among our Favorites this year. Known as a tough grader, his firm-but-always-honest approach has earned widespread respect. Our Egyptian, Siamese and Africat brothers and sisters have learned much about their culture in the well-established Afro-American Studies program. He illustrates boring lectures with his funny maps and wigs.

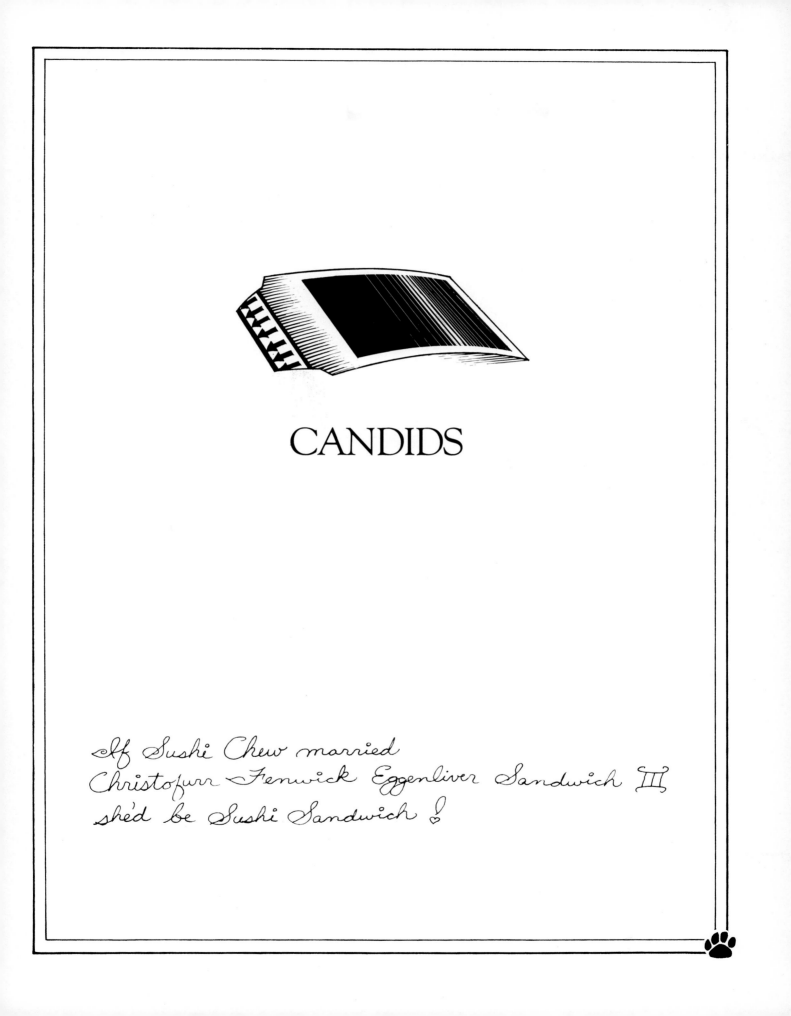

CANDIDS

If Sushi Chew married
Christofurr Fenwick Eggenliver Sandwich III
she'd be Sushi Sandwich ♡

If *I* turned in my exam the minute the lunch bell rang, *I* wouldn't get A's either.

Busy, well-educated Yearbook Editor and avid record collector Mark Mice spins the latest disc for another fascinated guest in his rec room.

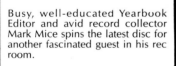

Welcome to our school. (Redo—will you get this damn hat off of me!)

Check this out. I'll ask her if I can buy her a drink.

Mr. Furbanks stands on a table to illustrate a point. Edsel is stunned by the fact that they're both wearing the same type of socks.

One step closer and you're tomorrow's dessert!

But we've always kept the rectal thermometers in the refrigerator.

Mike Redo pauses amidst his daily punishment to note Mr. Furbanks and Edsel are wearing the same socks.

Caveat emptor!

If you can't make it to class on time, Miss Parsley, why bother coming at all?

If you put a fish in one end, it comes out a bigger fish

Mike Redo—plane & simple.

Mark Mice and the Yearbook Staff take pride in announcing Lars Endicatt as this year's First Prize Winner in our Most Artistic Photo Award Contest for his sensitive portrait "Lulu's World."

Each year *Paw Prints* bestows only a few honorary awards. In the past the best cooks, seamstresses and interior designers have been recognized on these pages. But this year the Homer Formby Award for Excellence in Design goes to Jig Sawyer, who has designed and built a miniature replica of the town of Paw Paw.

SENIORS

If Katja Witdagütz married
Nelson Fish
she'd be Katja Fish.

PICTURED ABOVE LEFT TO RIGHT
FRONT ROW: Baxter Loveset, Cheryl Tigres, Edsel Knudsen, Catspurr Chatwick, Sophie McMeow, T.S. Alleycat,
      Eins Katzenjammer, Lulu Twitchfit
SECOND ROW: Eugene Fuzzerelli, Trixie Nixon, Tiger O'Malley, Zooey Furlinghetti, Zwei Katzenjammer, Cindy Tab, Lars Endicatt
THIRD ROW: Harmon Cronin, Abdul Catdabra, Canardly Telwat, Phyllis Snippitt, Chip Messeroffski, Chester Winchester,
      Oscar Hiss, Jig Sawyer
BACK ROW: Pyewacket Zoose, Albert Cheshire, Priscilla Pawsoff, Christofurr Fenwick, Eggenliver Sandwich III, Rufus Cubs,
      Pawpurr Van Purr Purr, Teresa Yikes
ABSENCES DUE TO:
Arbuckle, Oedipuss ♆; Beads, Rose ⊠; Beelzebub, Quentin ⊠; Betterborn, Chase Taylor ✝; Bootstraps, Earnest ♌; Chew, Sushi 🛒;
Chow, Alison ⌂; Crawfish, Joan ♒; Devereaux, Collin ⌂; Dweezle, Beasly ☁; Feleinberg, Eva ✝; Fish, Nelson ♌; Fluffnutter, Jane

24

▲; *Fumes, Berkeley* ⚶ ⚭; *Fur, Fred* ⚭; *Grouse, Emma* ☕; *Haddy, Finn N.* ⚒; *Housecat, Mary* ⚒; *Jones, Ntgabwe* ☁; *Katz, Kitty Tyler* ☕; *Khat, Chaka* ☕; *Kildecat, Curiosity* ⚓; *Kitta, Kunta* ☑; *Klinger, Stanley* ⚑; *Latigo, Spike* ☎; *Lick, Melvin* ☑; *Liverston, Stanley* ☎; *Lovecat, Sunshine* ⚒; *Lufter, Hobart* ☁; *Mackerel, Holly* ◊; *Mackerel, Wally* ⚑; *MacLeash, Clawford* ☕; *Madison, Pawline* ⚒; *Mange, Allen* ☎; *McPaws, Claws* ☁; *McWhiskers, Millicent* ⚭; *Mice, Mark* ⚐; *Mousehaus, Annemarie* ☕; *Nightingale, Mira* ✝; *Nosely, Agatha* ☎; *O'Ninetails, Catrine* ⚭; *Pawsano, Paloma* ⚶; *Purr, Sue* ⚭; *Quasar, Kirk* ⚶; *Ratatat, Stuart* ⚶; *Redo, Mike* ⚶; *Rizzo, Ratsy* ⚶; *Sandwich, Christofurr Fenwick Eggenliver III* ☕; *Smelts, Edna* ☁; *Squeeks, Waylon* ⚭; *Sturgeon, Nick* ☎; *Tirebiter, Felicia Faye* ⚒; *Tumi, Saki* ⚭; *Von Furstenbreed, Felicity* ▲; *Witdagütz, Kattja* ⚒; *Yung, Yin and Yang* ⚑ ◊; *Zooaster,*

KEY ⚓ = *gone fishing* ⚒ = *chasing cars* ☕ = *shopping at the Maul* ⚭ = *catnaps* ⚶ = *catnips* ☁ = *my dog ate the homework* ☑ = *my great-great-grandmother lost her ninth life* ⚑ = *showed up the next day* ◊ = *showed up the day before* ▲ = *pimple on nose leather* ✝ = *on an educational trip* ⚒ = *what picture?* ☎ = *too much to do* ⚐ = *yearbook duties*

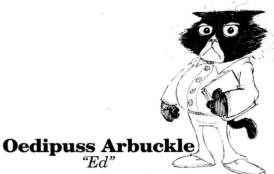

Oedipuss Arbuckle
"Ed"

"M is for the many things she gave me."

MORE THAN ONCE HEARD SAYING: "You mean I was supposed to bring a pencil to the exam?"
AMBITION: To make Mom purr-round
MOST LIKELY TO: Marry late
WILL ATTEND: Quiche-eater University
WE'LL REMEMBER: His clothes

Weejies from the rafters . . . fellas . . . ouch . . . couldn't claw his way out of a paper bag . . . skips rope . . . only child . . . an avid breather . . . scaredy cat . . . loves baths

ACTIVITIES: Stamp and Coin Collecting Club 3,4; Basket Weaving 4; Hypochondriacs Club 3,4; Turkey Club 3,4; Anglers 4

T.S. Alleycat
"Old Pussum"

"Unless one is a genius, it is best to be unintelligible."

AMBITION: To write the Great American Catbook
ROLE MODEL: Norman Meowler
FAVORITE BOOK: "Cat's Cradle"
PET PEEVE: Dangling participles
OFTEN HEARD SAYING: "The pen is mightier than the swordfish."
BEST TOPIC SENTENCE: "I never end my sentences a preposition with."
PERSONAL FANTASY: Nights at the round table as the Algonquin cat.

Nelson Fish might put it that way, but . . . that's a great idea for a book . . . the A team . . . High Society is literature's payoff . . . 10-letter words . . . have you read . . . manqué see, manqué do . . . darling of the mewses . . . esoteric is not a dirty word

ACTIVITIES: Editor, Litter 4; Quill and Claw 3,4; Contributing Editor, Scratching Post 4; Baseball Team 3,4; Pro and Conners 4; The Meowlers 4

gill — what can mere words say? everything. — T.S.!

CLASS CONUNDRUM

Quentin Beelzebub
"Digger"

"Lives are but a moment in time."

FAVORITE PHRASE: "Call the coroner."
FAVORITE GROUP: Grateful Dead
FAVORITE MOVIE: "Death Wish"
FAVORITE PART OF CLASS TRIP: Arlington Cemetery
SUMMER READING LIST: "No Exit," "Nausea," "Nine Deaths in Venice," "Been Down So Long It Looks Like Up To Me"
NOTED FOR: Negative Ions, Nicotine Stains

Life is a litter box . . . Chicken Little was right . . . menthol mind . . . death breath . . . Death Be Not Proud . . . downer

ACTIVITIES: Skull and Bones 1,2,3,4; Agatha Christie Club 1,2; H.P. Lovecraft 3; Edgar Allan Potpourris 4

Rose Beads
"Rose"

"What God intendeth seek not to divine: His plans for thee require no aid of thine."—Cato

AMBITION: To make it past purrgatory and collect $200
MOST LIKELY TO: Be born again and again
ROLE MODEL: Sister Mary Spade
FAVORITE SNACK: Sacramental wafers
REMEMBERED FOR: Scribbling crosses in her notebooks

Out of habit . . . learned her catechism . . . nun too pretty . . . nun too soon . . . nun too smart . . . nun of the above?

ACTIVITIES: Choir 2,3; Paw Paw Right to Litters 3,4; Bible Study 3,4

Dear Nelson,
you ARE a truly SENSitive CAt
And I PRAy that ONE DAy you
will KNOW God's TRUE LOVE.
Sincerely YouRs iN CHRISt
Rose Beads

Earnest Bootstraps
"Ernie-for-short"

"Make sure your key to success fits the ignition."

AMBITION: To be chaircat of Chicken of the Sea
ROLE MODEL: Cornelius Vandermilk
MOST LIKELY TO: Patent the *better* mousetrap
WE'LL REMEMBER: The cement scratching post fiasco
OFTEN HEARD SAYING: "An idea like this could be worth millions."
PET PEEVES: Taxes, especially that darn Fresh Tuna Tax

Make me an offer I can't refuse . . . three piece suits . . . busy, busy, busy . . . counts his change . . . it'll cost ya . . . organizer

ACTIVITIES: Young Investors 3,4; Young Republicats 3,4; Prom Committee 4; Junior Chamber of Commerce 3,4

Chase Taylor Betterborn
"Bucks"

"They say he's as rich as cream."

AMBITION: To stick to his own breed
ROLE MODEL: J. Pawl Getty
MOST LIKELY TO: Own stock in fish farms
WILL BE REMEMBERED FOR: His black-tie birthday party with goldfish for favors and Godiva chocolates in the shape of mice
FAVORITE TV SHOW: "Wall Street Week in Review"

Saturday afternoon manicures . . . if you have to ask how much, you can't afford it . . . why don't you try my tailor? . . . spats . . . Gucci with everything . . . I seem not to have anything smaller than a fifty . . . breeding is all . . . scented litter

ACTIVITIES: Junior Achievers 3,4; Breed-of-the-Month Club 4

Someday, I'll be rich enough to have a big picture like Abdul's

Chase

MOST POPULAR

This year Cat High has been very fortunate to have Abdul Catdabra from Saudi Arabia in its senior class. Often described as the ideal American Field Service student, he has brought an authentic enthusiasm for learning and experiencing life as we know it, as well as an eagerness to share his own caviar with us. We at CHS are proud of having had Abdul among us, not to mention his dad's petrodollars.

Dear my freind Nolsen, It is hope my that you will me visit in my cuontry. Yuors truly very, Abdul Catdabra

Abdul Catdabra
"Abacat"

"He that travels far knows much."

AMBITION: To own his own country
MOST LIKELY TO: Have nine wives
NEVER SEEN WITHOUT: His mat pointing towards Mecca
WILL REMEMBER: Arguments with Eva Feleinberg over the Purrsian Gulf
FIRST WORDS IN ENGLISH: "It's sex o'clock."
FAVORITE SONG: "I Ran"—Flock of Seagulls

CLOSE SECOND: "Abra Catdabra"—Steve Miller
PET PEEVE: The Purrmian Basin
Your bread is so thick! . . . baba ghanouj is *not* ground mice! . . . you know what this place needs? sand . . . in my country
ACTIVITIES: AFS Student 4; If It's Worth Doing It's Worth Doing Well Club 4

Albert Cheshire
"The Big A"

"Purr softly and carry a big stick."

AMBITION: To win a Rhodes Collarship
MOST LIKELY TO: Have his picture on a Wheaties box
WE'LL REMEMBER: 98-yard touchdown run against Rooster Tech
FAVORITE BOOK: Writings of Catfucius
FAVORITE MOVIE: "The Seventh Seal"
OFTEN HEARD SAYING: "No thanks, Manx."

Ladies cat . . . one at a time, girls . . . brains *and* brawn . . . hey, cool it . . . BCOC . . . Harvard bound . . . Mr. Everything

ACTIVITIES: Football 2,3,4; Supper Club 3,4; Prom Committee 4

Catspurr Chatwick
"The Little Professor"

"You can look it up if you want, but I know I'm right."

AMBITION: To be mayor of Paw Paw
MOST LIKELY TO: Be mayor of Paw Paw
FAVORITE BOOK: "How to Pull Your Own String"
FAVORITE MOVIE: "All the President's Cats"
WILL REMEMBER: Stuffing ballots till dawn
OFTEN HEARD SAYING: "Ask not what Cat High can do for you but what you can do for Cat High"

Mr. Versatility . . . point of order . . . a real diplocat . . . never short for words . . . invoking Robert's Rules . . . a canary in every pot . . . I don't think the faculty's so bad . . . being the mayor's son just gives me that much more experience

ACTIVITIES: Student Council President 4; Band 1,2,3,4; Paw Paw Clean Up Booster 4; Meowlers 1,2,3,4; Baseball 3,4; Honor Society 3,4; Chess Team 4; Diplocats 4

Alison Chow
"Whiz"

"The square of the hypotemouse is equal to the sum of the square of the other two sides."—Pythagorat

AMBITION: To complete the Chow theorem
FAVORITE SONG: "Lucky Number"
FAVORITE BOOK: "Advanced Catculus"
FAVORITE LANGUAGES: Basic and Pawtran
ROLE MODEL: Mr. Bandersnatch
OFTEN HEARD SAYING: "Log me in, Mr. B."
WE'LL REMEMBER: Her appetite for chalk
CLASS TRIP LEGACY: Digit goes to Washington

Walking computer . . . no. 2 pencils . . . future Nobel Prize runner-up . . . sharp as a tack . . . let me explain catculus, Abdul . . . gotta study, bye

ACTIVITIES: Mathletes 3,4; The Numerals 1,2; Sines For a Better Society 1,2; The Whiz and Proofs 1,2,3,4

Sushi Chew
"Muffy," "Binky," "Buffy," "Mimsy"
"Pink and green are always in."
—Lily Pawlitzer

PET PEEVE: To be called by her real name
FAVORITE MOVIE: "Love Story"
FAVORITE BOOK: "Love Story"
FAVORITE SONG: "Theme from Love Story"
FAVORITE ACTRESS: Alley McGraw

Madras on Monday . . . buy in coordinates . . . 20 pairs of espadrilles . . . hopes to live in Greenwich . . . summer on Nantukcat . . . monogram it! . . . you call *that* a yacht!

ACTIVITIES: Field Mouse Hockey 1,2,3,4; Volleymice 3,4

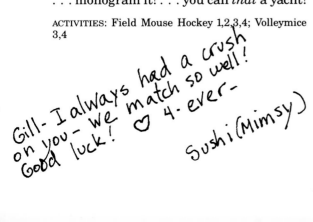

Gill- I always had a crush on you - we match so well! Good luck! ♡ 4-ever-
—Sushi (Mimsy)

Joan Crawfish
"Jay Jay"

"Being a painter, I address myself first to visual sensation . . . and the pursuit of mice."

ROLE MODEL: Marcel Duchats
FAVORITE ARTISTIC DEVICE: Cubist mice
FAVORITE MOVIE: "Un Chien Andalou"
WILL BE REMEMBERED FOR: Her famous kinetic fish-sculpture installation in the library
OFTEN HEARD SAYING: "Art is anti-destiny."

Rodin not rodent . . . Dada dearest . . . mouse models . . . squirrel brushes are best . . . expressing the tender, the luscious, the edible . . . the shark at the bottom of the pool and the mouse holes in the principal's office

ACTIVITIES: Mouse of the Month Calendar 3,4; Paw Paw Dada 3,4; Tasteful Palettes 1,2,3,4; Homecoming Decorations Committee 3,4; Prom Decorations Committee 2,3,4

Harmon Cronin
"Professor 'Croonin' Cronin"
"Mewsic is the eye of the ear."

ROLE MODEL: Luciano Pawvarati
MOST LIKELY TO: Return to Cat High as a mewsic teacher
WILL ALWAYS REMEMBER: Sophie McMeow's sweet soprano
PET PEEVE: Cats who yowl off key
FAVORITE DEBATE STANCE: It is not the case that you should leave it to Beaver.
OFTEN HEARD SAYING: "E,G,B,D,F, Sophie (every good bass deserves favors)"

High C, not me . . . notes to you . . . that's mewsic to my errors . . . it goes like this . . . if mewsic be the food of love, play on

ACTIVITIES: Meowlers 2,3,4; Purr-A-Thon Leader 2,3,4; Yowls and Screamers 1; Baseball 2,3,4; Pro and Conners 3,4

When you talk about this and you will keep it funny! Collin

Collin Devereaux
"Catfuscious"

"Humor is wit with a rooster's tail feathers stuck in its cap."

AMBITION: To write a humor book about computer software
MOST LIKELY TO: Wanna buy a duck
FAVORITE MOVIE: The Manx Brothers' "Animal Crackers"
FAVORITE BOOK: "Archie and Mehitabel"
ROLE MODEL: Rich Litter

Impurrsonations . . . the kippers caper . . . I've got your number . . . have you heard the one about? . . . ha, ha, ha . . . I'm not kidding

ACTIVITIES: Funny Button Club 1,2; Cool Tie Club 3; Mathletes 3,4; Cool Button and Funny Tie Club 4

Rufus Cubs
"Cubby"

"Diamonds are forever."

ROLE MODEL: Catfish Hunter
FAVORITE BOOK: "The Umpire Strikes Back"
OFTEN HEARD SAYING: "Do we have a scouting report on that guy?"
FAVORITE MOVIE: "Damn Yankees"
CUBS LEGACY: Mickey Mantle book report used from 4th to 12th grade
WE'LL REMEMBER: The grass stains on his pants, the dirt under his eyes, chewing catnip in the dugout
MOST LIKELY TO: Slide home

Hum it in there, Harmon . . . good game . . . what are the odds, Nick? . . . nice try . . . I'd really love to take that make-up test after school, Miss Parsely, but I have to go to practice . . . bang the drum slowly, Catspurr . . . bad news, bears . . . good effort

ACTIVITIES: Batboy 1; Baseball 2,3,4; Hoopers 2,3,4; Football 2,3,4; Catfish Hunters 3,4

Lars Endicatt
"The Fixer"

"A picture is worth a thousand dollars."

FAVORITE SONG: "Kodachrome"
FAVORITE PHOTOGRAPHER: "Cattier Bresson
FAVORITE MOVIE: "Blow up"
IDEA OF A GOOD TIME ON A SATURDAY NIGHT: Going to the darkroom and seeing what develops
OFTEN HEARD SAYING: "That drives me up a tree."
WILL BE REMEMBERED FOR: Falling out of a tree

Watch the birdie . . . documentary of D.C. . . . tri-pawwed . . . those pre-debate confurrences with Trixie Nixon . . . say cheese . . . just hold that position a second longer, Lulu, while I adjust the apurrture

ACTIVITIES: Pro and Conners 3,4; Photography Club 2,3,4; Bird Watchers Club 3,4; Yearbook Photography Editor 4

Beasley Dweezle
"Blaze"

"A winner never quits, and a quitter is never late for lunch."

MOST LIKELY TO: Skip classes between meals
AMBITION: To buy into a Lord-of-the-Chickens franchise
WILL BE REMEMBERED FOR: His own personal truant officer
PHILOSOPHY: College is for the birds.
OFTEN HEARD SAYING: "T.G.I.F."
LAST HEARD SAYING: "Paws don't fail me now."

You're bad, jump up and get it . . . an unforgettable jump shot . . . I'm outa here

ACTIVITIES: Hoopers 2,3,4

Eva Feleinberg
"Miss Agosh"

"The second coming *and* the second helping."

ROLE MODEL: Golda Meow
AMBITION: To run a kitbutz
FAVORITE BOOK: "Go Wild With Gefilte Fish: A Thousand Recipes"
FAVORITE AUTHOR: Elie Weasel
FAVORITE SONG: "Exodus"
FAVORITE MOVIE: "The Meshugana Professor"
FAVORITE TESTAMENT: The Old One
PET PEEVE: Mixed marriages ("I like Abdul but we could never be close")
DREAM DATE: Nelson Fish on Friday

Eat, you'll feel better . . . chicken soup . . . next year in Jerusalem . . . thanks to the fishing team for retrieving my bas mitzvah shawl . . . knish and fish in the cateteria!

ACTIVITIES: Prom Refreshment Committee 3,4; Zionist Lioness Club 3,4; Matzoh Makers of America 3,4; Goldsmith Club 2,3,4

Nelson Fish
"Gill"

"I'm a lousy writer, but a helluva lot of cats have got lousy taste."

AMBITION: To run a small publishing house
COLLEGE CHOICE: Oxfurred University
WILL ATTEND: Yaowle
FAVORITE BOOKS: Too numerous to mention
FAVORITE MOVIE: They are never as good as the book
WE'LL REMEMBER: His modeling for Cattymoiselle
MOST LIKELY TO: Have a "Fish" wife
OFTEN HEARD SAYING: Just one more rewrite
PET PEEVE: The writing of T.S. Alleycat

Bitten by the Fish . . . doubtless . . . covercat . . . hand me the Wite-out . . . 55 w.p.m. . . . the fine print . . . the index . . . an illegible pawprint

ACTIVITIES: Hieroglyphics Club 2,3,4; Key Ticklers 1,2; Corrasables 3; Litterary Society 3,4; The Litter Contributing Editor 3,4

Keep the faith   Eva

Berkeley Fumes
"Bogart"

"What a long strange trip it's been."
—Grateful Dead

AMBITION: To be a pharmacist
FAVORITE SUBJECT: Chemistry
ROLE MODELS: Hunter S. Thomcat and Ken Cheesy
OFTEN HEARD SAYING: "What? I mean, could you please stand still? You're spinning."
COLLEGE CHOICE: Very undecided

Surf's up! . . . Paw Paw Purple . . . quick, bury it in the kitty litter! . . . but, officer, what could possibly interest you about my little herb garden?

ACTIVITIES: Bong-a-thon Solicitor 2,3; Bong Team Captain 3,4; Anglers 4; Getting By On Getting By 1,2,3,4

Jane Fluffnutter
"Complain Jane"

"I'd prefer it in a slightly lighter shade of fuchsia."

AMBITION: To get satisfaction
MOST LIKELY TO: Get no satisfaction
ROLE MODEL: Mrs. Whiner
OFTEN HEARD SAYING: "Waiter, there's a fly in my soup!"
OFTEN SEEN: Crying over spilt milk

Here come da judge . . . Whhhyyy not? . . . the walking catastrophe . . . wait up! . . . stop cheating off my paper!!!

ACTIVITIES: Examining Cateteria Food for Cat Hairs and Whiskers 1,2,3,4; Washing the Blackboard Between Classes 2,3,4; Purrfectionists 3,4

Do I know you? Bogie?

HIGHEST MOST

Zooey Furlinghetti
"Beat"
"Picture yourself in a boat on a river, With tangerine trees and marmalade skies"—The Beatles

AMBITION: To jam with Cat Metheny and Mangy Chuckione
WILL BE REMEMBERED FOR: That crazy saxophone
OFTEN HEARD SAYING: "That's so cool it's Arctic."

How's the harvest coming, Berkeley? . . . let's get Catman Crothers for the prom! . . . but, Miss Maps, the light hurts my eyes . . . Muddy Waters . . . involved but understated

ACTIVITIES: Baseball 3,4; Football 2,3,4; Acousticats Combo 3; Dreadwhiskers 4

Fred Fur
"Freddy," "Mr. Nice Guy"
"A smile is a curve that sets things straight."

FAVORITE SONGS: "Everything is Beautiful," "Isn't She Lovely?," "My Favorite Things"
ROLE MODEL: The cat from Glad
FAVORITE ACTIVITIES: Homework, recreation, cathletics, eating, sleeping, earning an honest dollar
OFTEN HEARD SAYING: "You girls need a ride?" "You guys need a ride?"
PET PEEVE: Pet peeves
FAVORITE MOVIE: "Three cats in the Fountain," "It's a Wonderful Life," "Heaven Can Wait"
FAVORITE BOOK SERIES: "Just So Stories"

Anything I can do to help? . . . have a nice day . . . Olivia Newton John T-shirts . . . Henny Penny should have shared . . . goody two paws

ACTIVITIES: Pawsitive Thinkers 1,2,3,4; Teacher's Petters 2,3; Bus Patrol 3,4; Cub Scouts 3,4; Litter Box Patrol 1,2,3,4

MOST PURRSUASIVE

Emma Grouse
"Slim"

"Two mice converged in a wood
and I
I ate the fatter one,
and that has made all the difference."
—Robert Furrost

OFTEN HEARD SAYING: "Did you want that piece?"
MOST LIKELY TO: Have just one more bite.
WILL REMEMBER: All you can eat for $5.95
FAVORITE BOOK: "Thirty Days to a Better Bottom"
FAVORITE OPERA: "Aïda"
WE'LL REMEMBER: Her edible complex

Oh, boy, chocolate mouse! . . . plop, plop, fizz, fizz . . . move over

ACTIVITIES: Bake Sale Committee 2,3; Diners Club 1,2,3,4; Lunch Room Monitor 2,3,4; Prom Refreshment Acquisition Committee 3,4; Tuna Club on Wheat 3,4; Weight Watchers Club 2,3, Vice President 4

Eugene Fuzzerelli
"Slugger"

"Good things come in six-packs."

FAVORITE MOVIE: "Road Warrior"
FAVORITE BOOK: "Zen and the Art of Motorcycle Maintenance"
PET PEEVES: School
NOTED FOR: His purrsuasive powers
WE'LL NEVER FORGET: The time he took the principal hostage

Come with me to the Catsbar . . . the panty raid . . . better to burn out than to rust . . . my paw and your face . . . big bike . . . I never let school interfere with my education

ACTIVITIES: Band 4; Football 1,2,3,4; Cat High Chapter Leader, Little Dickens Motorcycle Club 4; Mouse Patrol Captain 4

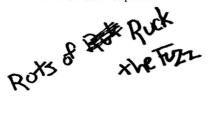

Rots of ~~Bull~~ Ruck the Fuzz

Oscar Hiss
"Catloaf"

"For those about to rock, we salute you."
—AC/DC

AMBITION: To collect bats for Ozzie Osbourne
MOST LIKELY TO: Bring the heavy metal underground out of the closet
FAVORITE SONG: "Like a Cat Out of Hell"
FAVORITE BAND: Meowly Hatchet
FAVORITE MOVIE: "Rock and Roll High School"
MEWSIC TO HIS EARS: Feedback
PET PEEVE: Cat Boone

Leather bracelets . . . distortion! . . . I don't need no wa wa . . . Def Leopard 4-ever . . . Inna Gadda Davida . . . we need more lead guitars!

ACTIVITIES: Heavy Metal Shop 3,4; Prom Entertainment Advisor 4

Finn N. Haddy
"Mutter"

"If you can't beat 'em, join 'em."

FAVORITE ACTIVITY: Chasing cars with Felicia Faye Tirebiter
ROLE MODEL: Al Poochino
MOST LIKELY TO: Embarrass his mother
FAVORITE MOVIE: "Dog Day Afternoon"
FAVORITE BOOK: "No Bad Dogs"
WE'LL REMEMBER: His dogged curiosity
SECRET DESIRE: His own hydrant

Hey, they're not so bad . . . hair of the dog that bit you . . . try it, you'll like it . . . very fetching . . . here are your slippers, Felicia

ACTIVITIES: Milk Bones 2,3,4; Repeal-the-Leash-Law Committee 3,4; Heartworm Fund Booster 3; Bay-at-the-Moon Club 2,3

Ntgabwe Jones
"Alphabet"

"When you notice a cat in profound meditation, the reason, I tell you, is always the same: his mind is engaged in a rapt contemplation of the thought of the thought, of his name: his ineffable effable effanineffable deep and inscrutable singular name."
—Tabby S. Eliot

MOST LIKELY TO: Change his name
AMBITION: To climb all the way to the top of his family tree
FAVORITE BOOK: "The Cat in the Hat Is Black"
FAVORITE DRINK: Roots beer
FAVORITE SONG: "Paint It Black"
PET PEEVE: Jive turkeys
WE'LL REMEMBER: Soul food on ice

Champale . . . Chatwick, what a pigmy . . . don't jive me, man . . . guess who's coming to dinner . . . Kunta, how do we spell Tanganyika?

ACTIVITIES: Genealogist's Club 3,4; History Club 4

Gill—
—If you're having a party, I'll make the dessert.
Mary

Mary Housecat
"Mary Housecat, Mary Housecat"
"Everybody needs a mouse-o-matic."

FAVORITE SUBJECT: Home Economics
FAVORITE SONG: "Stand By Your Man"
FAVORITE SINGER: Loratta Lynn
FAVORITE BOOK: "The Total Feline" by Marabel Morgan
SUMMER READING: Sillypet Romances
ROLE MODEL: Betty Cracker
PET PEEVE: Toms who don't know how to slice Thanksgiving mice
WILL BE REMEMBERED FOR: Purrfect patterns for cat's pajamas
MOST LIKELY TO: Throw in the sponge
FAVORITE T.V. SHOW: "The Happy Homemaker"

Those colorful pawtholders . . . knows the way to a tom's heart . . . country catseroles . . . garage sales . . . candidate for MRS degree . . . wardrobe by Talbots

ACTIVITIES: Bake Sale Committee 3,4; Creative Cleaning 4; Catnip Madness Pamphleteer 3,4

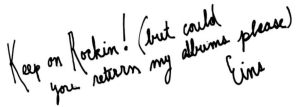

Keep on Rockin! (but could you return my albums please) Eins

Eins Katzenjammer
"Itchy"

"Shouldn't the whole world be dancing?"

MOST LIKELY TO: Get dance fever
FAVORITE ACTRESS: Jennifurr Beals
FAVORITE BAND: The Stray Cats
FAVORITE ACTIVITY: Hitch-hiking to
Minniemousapolis
PET PEEVE: Fleas

Hubba hubba, Bubba . . . made a killing in
the flea market . . . I'm the pick of the litter
. . . paws de deux . . . let's boogie . . . it goes
like this

ACTIVITIES: Baseball 3,4; Football 2,3,4; Pepcats 3,4;
Prom Entertainment Committee 4; Flea Circus
Ringmaster 4

Kitty Tyler Katz
"Kitten"

"A good coat is worth a thousand licks."

AMBITION: Six-figure dating
MOST LIKELY TO: Charge it to Daddy.
FAVORITE BOOK: "Princess Daisy"
OFTEN HEARD SAYING: "That'd be oodles of
fun."
FAVORITE THING IN THE WHOLE WORLD:
Fred Fur, Chase Betterborn, Mr. Furbanks
WILL BE REMEMBERED FOR: Those heart-
shaped glasses

String of pearls . . . are you sure it's
kosher? . . . claret claw polish . . . I do *not*
dye my whiskers

ACTIVITIES: Ratterettes 2,3; Pussycats 3,4; Pepcats
3,4

DEAR GILL
  I'M SO SORRY ABOUT THAT DATE
SOPH. YEAR BUT MY FUR REALLY
WAS FILTHY, I SWEAR!
            KITTY
      P.S. CALL ME!

Chaka Khat
"Val"

"Glow, c'mon glow, the funky purrty flame in my cat heart."—The Beach Cats

AMBITION: To learn to surf
MOST LIKELY TO: Move to the San Furrnando Alley
OFTEN HEARD SAYING: "Like, gag me with a 2-in-1 collar."
SUMMER READING: "Vogue"
FAVORITE ACTIVITY: Writing poetry on charge slips
WE'LL REMEMBER: Her letter from Moon Unit
SECRET DESIRE: To domesticate Spike Latigo

Alley Girl . . . fur sure . . . your claws are grody . . . totally . . . to the manx . . . short skirts in every season . . . let's dance to some meaningless music

ACTIVITIES: Pep Club 2,3,4; Polka Dot Club 3,4

Zwei Katzenjammer
"Ditto"

"We have met the enemy and he is us."

AMBITION: To write the definitive biography of Eins Katzenjammer
ROLE MODEL: Tommy Smothers
PET PEEVE: Being called the Katzenjammer Kids
WILL BE REMEMBERED FOR: Having a wardrobe exactly like Eins Katzenjammer
MOST LIKELY TO: Be mistaken for his brother

Anybody got any Doublemint? . . . no, you're *not* seeing double . . . hates mirrors

ACTIVITIES: Copycats 1; Ditto Club 2, President 3,4; Mimeo Monitors 3,4; The Litter 1,2,3,4

Have a great year! (but could you please return my brother's albums)
Zwei

Kunta Kitta
"Kooky"

"It's a jungle out there."

AMBITION: To return to his roots
DESTINY: To go corporate
WE'LL REMEMBER: The Back-to-Africat Movement
OFTEN HEARD SAYING: "How do you spell Zimbabwe, Ntgabwe!"
FAVORITE BOOK: "Soul on Mice"
MOTTO: All cats are gray in the dark.

Wanna watusi? . . . I've got rhythm . . . deep voice . . . black cats are *not* bad luck

ACTIVITIES: Good Luck Society 1,2,3,4; Alex Haley Fan Club 3,4; Hoopers 1,2,3,4

Curiosity Kildecat
"Lovey"

"Speak to me only with thine eyes, and I will pledge with mine."

OVERHEARD SAYING: "He looked like an Egyptian god. I don't think he knew more than ten words—'trust me' and maybe one or two more."
ALSO OVERHEARD SAYING: "Hello . . . oh, hi Tiger. No, I'm not doing anything special. No, my mother's at the movies with a friend. Uh huh. You're terrible! No, I couldn't. CLICK . . . Are you still there?"
PET PEEVE: Boys (once a day)
WILL REMEMBER: Spike Latigo's romantic catpitulations
FAMOUS FOR: The innocent eyes with the Big Meow
COLLEGE CHOICE: The Sorbonne (but will attend Livercliff Junior College)
MOST LIKELY TO: Get hurt

A real belle . . . save me the last dance . . . thousand-volt eyes . . . taffeta and jeans . . . be gentle

ACTIVITIES: Homecoming Candidate 4

CLASS CHAUFFEUR

And, I hope you'll never forget me! Stan

Stanley Klinger
"Go-fur"

"Ask not what your friends can do for you, but what you can do for your friends."

AMBITION: To find a bunch of guys who dress alike and follow them around.
MOST LIKELY TO: Find those guys
OFTEN HEARD SAYING: "Hey, guys, wait up."
FAVORITE CARD GAME: Fifty-two Pick Up
WE'LL REMEMBER: His dad's convertible

So should I meet you later? . . . my invitation must've gotten lost in the mail . . . youngest in class (skipped a grade) . . . ok, you can use the car, but this is the last time

ACTIVITIES: Mathletes 4; Football Manager 1,2,4; Track Manager 1,2,4; Teacher's Petters 1,2,4; Spirit Week Litter Chairman 4; Lunch Bell Ringer 4

Edsel Knudsen
"Mr. Gizmo"

"There's no time like the present to the 10th decimal place."

ROLE MODEL: Carl Sagan
WILL REMEMBER: Breaking his glasses while *watching* a football game!
OFTEN HEARD SAYING: "Hey, Redo, what's the joke du jour?"
FAVORITE SONG: "She Blinded Me with Science"
SATURDAY NIGHT DATE: A floppy disc
PET PEEVE: Computers made in Japan

Sardine eater . . . does not compute, Will Robinson . . . pre-professional . . . a rare collection of hormones . . . 256K! . . . CAT scores 008/799 . . . brain food

ACTIVITIES: Slide Rulers 1; Discs and Chips 2,3,4; Buttons, Knobs and Widgets 2,3,4; Honor Society 4; Football Team 3,4; Computer Club 2,3,4

BEST DRESSED

Melvin Lick
"Mr. Unnatural"

"I just want you to love me, primal doubts and all."—Paddy Chayefsky

AMBITION: To go to State
DESTINY: Junior College
MOST LIKELY TO: Default on his student loan
WE SUSPECT: His mother makes his clothes
OFTEN HEARD SAYING: "Well, can't you wash your hair some other night?"
THINKS: Roll call is a snack

Responsible for letting Edna Smelts out of the bag . . . hates being called "Animal" . . . always last called . . . always last picked . . . a reputation built on rumor

ACTIVITIES: Experimental Lab Subject 3,4; Science Fiction Club Secretary 4; Strange Dream Club 3,4

Spike Latigo
"Spike"

"What are you looking at, flea-bag?"

FAVORITE BOOK: "On the Road"
FAVORITE MOVIE: "Easy Rider"
FAVORITE SONG: "Born to Ride"
FAVORITE SUBJECT: Metal shop
AMBITION: To define 5th gear
WILL REMEMBER: Being suspended for smoking in the litter box
NOTED FOR: Missing right eye (although *we* the editors, didn't notice anything wrong)

Future Hell's Angel . . . don't lean *against* the turn! . . . Altamont, what a trip to have been there! . . . violated the dress code more times than he has lives . . . how about that date with Catrine O'Ninetails?! . . . main squeeze—Chaka Khat

ACTIVITIES: Dirt Bike Derby 1,2,3,4; Metal Shop 3,4; Cat High Chapter, Hell's Little Dickens 3,4; Baseball 3,4

Stanley Liverston
"Dr. Stan"

"Physician, heal thy cat."

ROLE MODEL: Dr. Dolittle
AMBITION: To be chief of staff at the Meow Clinic
PET OPERATION: To separate the Siamese Twins
MOST LIKELY TO: Flunk organic chemistry
DESTINY: To sell insurance
OFTEN HEARD SAYING: "There's more than one way to cure a cat."

The eternal pre-med . . . say ah . . . a spoonful of catnip helps the medicine go down . . . Dr. Liverston I presume . . . who barfed in my lab book? . . . dissecting mice . . . started preparing for the MCATs in 7th grade

ACTIVITIES: Vet Clinic Volunteer 3,4; Mixed Chorus 3,4 (it'll look good on my record)

Sunshine Lovecat
"Sunny"

"Mine is the sunlight, mine is the morning."—Cat Stevens

AMBITION: To bring peace and joy to the world with as little effort as possible
ROLE MODELS: Zonker Harris, Maynard G. Krebs
FAVORITE SINGER: Donovan
FAVORITE ALBUM: "Teaser and the Firecat"
OFTEN HEARD SAYING: "It's meaningful, but can it be done lying out on the grass?"
FAVES: Pop art, pop tarts, pop tops, patches, paisley, embroidery sandals, incense, head shops
MOST LIKELY TO: Own a chain of music and novelty shops

Hates RATC . . . that's soo relevant . . . early action Hampster College . . . pawsing to sniff the flowers

ACTIVITIES: Love-Ins For The Wealthy 3,4; Art Club 2,3

Sorry you missed the Sunrise watching this spring! peace now Sunshine

Hobart Lufter
"Hobiecat"

"I don't want tunas with good taste, I want tunas that taste good."

ROLE MODEL: The Pussycat
AMBITION: To go to sea with an owl
MOST LIKELY TO: Own a pea-green boat
DESTINY: To have honey and plenty of money
BEEN SEEN: Eating with a runcible spoon
IDEA OF A GOOD TIME ON A SATURDAY NIGHT: Dancing hand in hand on the edge of the sand by the light of the moon

Saturday chess games on the Catamaran . . . turkey on the hill . . . clams on the half-shell . . . let's sail to Mackincat! . . . ahoy . . . 13 buttons on his trousers (count 'em, Curiosity!) . . . coming about

ACTIVITIES: Piggywig Club 1,2,3,4; Chess Club 3,4; Popeye Fan Club 2,3

Baxter Loveset
"Ace"

"Game, set, match."

AMBITION: Big bucks on the pro-tennis circuit
DESTINY: Tennis elbows (4)
FAVORITE SONG: "Hey, Hey, You, You, Get Off of My Court."
PET PEEVES: Paw faults, cat gut
OFTEN HEARD SAYING: "Tennis is a game of stroking, not hitting."
WE'LL REMEMBER: Licking John MacEnfido (on the court, that is)

Top cat on the tennis team . . . rough or smooth? . . . late nights at Sophie McMeow's . . . hey—Soph and I were just talking strategy . . . leading protest at the racquet-string factory

ACTIVITIES: Tennis 1,2,3,4; Cat Gut Your Tongue 3,4; Baseball 2,3,4

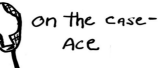

on the case—
Ace

Some people sign up → Some people sign down → But ME, I'm different. I sign around!

Wally Mackerel
"Mumbles"

"For a fish without a fin, there's a fowl without a feather."

MOST LIKELY TO: Stay in Paw Paw
ROLE MODEL: Walter Mitty
FAVORITE BOOK: "The Quiet One"
FAVORITE SONG: "Sounds of Silence"
FAVORITE FOOD: Mystery Fish
WE'LL REMEMBER: The day Wally spoke
WHAT HE SAID: "But Miss Parsely, I've never *been* absent."

Who is that guy in the third roe? . . . has designer genes . . . the secret life of Wally Mackerel . . . Mack the nerd . . . quiet as a mouse

ACTIVITIES: Anglers 3,4; Library Club 4; Rest Period Monitor 3; Lunch Bell Polisher 1; Lunch Bell Repair 2; Lunch Bell Ringer 3,4

HOLLY

Holly Mackerel
"Dotty"

"Poetry is to me as song is to others."

NEVER SEEN WITHOUT: A pen, a pad, and a smile
FAVORITE BOOK: "Old Possum's Book of Practical Cats"
OFTEN HEARD SAYING: "He's my brother, and he's o.k."
POETRY PRIZE: Someday I'll be a poet,
I want everyone to know it,
I'm clever and I'm cute,
I write poetry to boot,
My future is all set,
I'll be successful, yup,
you bet!

She's WHOSE sister??? . . . dreams of T.S. Alleycat . . . everybody's friend . . . love poems to T.S. (they were pretty good, too!)

ACTIVITIES: Litter 2,3,4; Polka Dot Club 3, President 4

Pawline Madison
"Dolly"
"You can never be too rich or too slinky."
—The Duchpuss of Windsor

SUMMER READING: "Town & Country"
ROLE MODEL: Jackie Onasshiss
AMBITION: To have a ballroom
FAVORITE SONG: "The Blue Danube Waltz"
PET PEEVE: Fuzzerelli's awful table manners
OFTEN HEARD SAYING: "Darling, *every* cat should know when to use a fish-fork."

Best salmon mousse . . . hostess with the mostess . . . wearing *what* to the front door??? . . . catered sockhops . . . designer collars . . . kissing the air

ACTIVITIES: Tea Pouring 3,4; Dinner Partyers 3,4; Prom Interior Decoration 4

Clawford MacLeash
"Red"
"From each according to his ability, to each according to his fleas."—Karl Manx

AMBITION: To radicalize Cat High janitorial staff
WILL BE REMEMBERED FOR: Painting a hammer-and-sickle on the principal's Catillac
LOVES: Working cats
HATES: Fat cats
OFTEN HEARD SAYING: "Morris bites."
BRINGS NEW MEANING TO WORDS: "Get off my case."
VOTED: Least likely to succeed

Tsar struck . . . always shares lunch . . . avoids drafts . . . smile on your brother . . . comes the revolution

ACTIVITIES: Paw Paw Socialists 3; Paw Paw Communists 4; Young Spartacus League 1,2,3,4; Cats Ostracizing Morris Outwardly (head picketer) 3,4

When you sit under the paw paw tree, close your eyes and think of me, Pawline

Sorry you were never fast enough to catch up. Sophie

Sophie McMeow
"Sophisticat"

"Travel is *so* broadening."

FAVORITE MOVIE: "Cousin, Cousine"
OFTEN HEARD SAYING: "C'est les vies"
FAVORITE MUSIC: Pawchebel's Canon
DESTINY: To have a French chef
FAVORITE ACTIVITY: Shopping on the Champs Elysalley
WILL BE REMEMBERED FOR: Her authentic Purrisian accent
MOST LIKELY TO: Have a pied-à-terre
OFTEN SPOTTED: *Harmon*izing—Yuk, yuk

Oh, Harmon, I'd love to . . . les affaires du coeur . . . life in the fast lane . . . mixed doubles aprés-midi . . . pajama parties . . . a one-cat sorority . . . organizer . . . that's a circumflex, not a . . .

ACTIVITIES: Pussycats 2,3,4; Language Club 3,4; Meowlers 2,3,4; Prom Queen 4; Tennis 1,2,3,4

Allen Mange
"Asbury"

"What else can we do now except roll down the windows and let the wind blow back our fur?"

AMBITION: To be the Boss for a while
MOST LIKELY TO: Live in Jungleland
STUCK ON: Rose Beads
OFTEN HEARD SAYING: "She's the one."
FAVORITE SONG: "Catillac Ranch"
PET PEEVE: Growin' up
BEST MEDICAL EXCUSE: The Fever

I came for you . . . magic rat . . . New Jersey bound . . . born to run . . . the river

ACTIVITIES: Radio Club 3,4; Future D.J.s of America 4

MOST CHASED

Millicent McWhiskers
"Milly"

"There is only one kind of love, but there are a thousand imitations."

AMBITION: To know *everybody*
MOST LIKELY TO: Live her lives to the manx
ROLE MODELS: Lois Lane, Amelia Earhart
FAVORITE BOOK: Any Nancy Drew
FAVORITE T.V. SHOW: "The Wild Kingdom"

Leave it to Milly . . . a reporter's nose for news . . . early decision Bryn Meower College . . . not interested in any of the Toms because she knows too much about them . . .

ACTIVITIES: Homeroom President 3,4; The Scratching Post 2,3,4; Nine Lifers 3,4

Claws McPaws
"Knuckles"

"Nice guys finish last."—Lion Durocher

AMBITION: To kick sand in Charles Atlas's face
MOST LIKELY TO: Survive
FAVORITE BROADWAY PLAY: "Maim"
FAVORITE BOOK: "Real Cats Eat Raw Mice"
ROLE MODEL: Clint Eastcat
OFTEN HEARD SAYING: "O.K., then I'll break *both* your kneecaps."

Picks a mean lock . . . loves crossing other's paths . . . tailchaser . . . turned down once by a feline (what *was* her name?)

ACTIVITIES: Detention 1,2,3,4; Jail 5; Billy Club 2,3,4

Sorry 'bout the black eye.
Claws

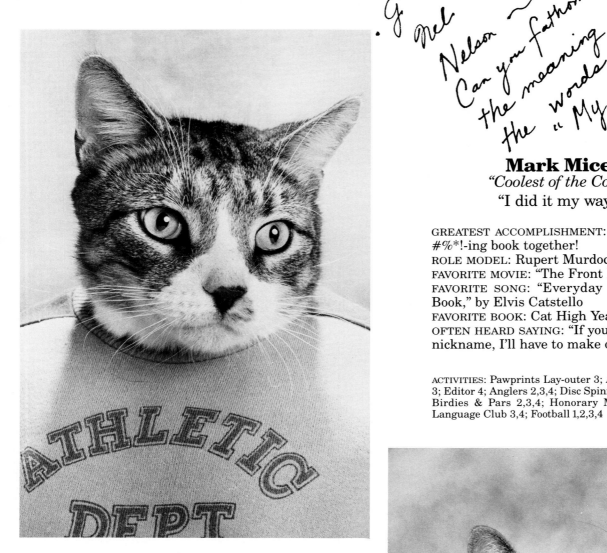

G. Nel — Nelson — Can you fathom the meaning of the words "My book is out?" What a groove — Mark

Mark Mice
"Coolest of the Cool"
"I did it my way."

GREATEST ACCOMPLISHMENT: Putting this #%*!-ing book together!
ROLE MODEL: Rupert Murdoch
FAVORITE MOVIE: "The Front Page"
FAVORITE SONG: "Everyday I Write The Book," by Elvis Catstello
FAVORITE BOOK: Cat High Yearbook
OFTEN HEARD SAYING: "If you don't have a nickname, I'll have to make one up."

ACTIVITIES: Pawprints Lay-outer 3; Assistant Editor 3; Editor 4; Anglers 2,3,4; Disc Spinners 3,4; Eagles, Birdies & Pars 2,3,4; Honorary Mensa member; Language Club 3,4; Football 1,2,3,4

Chip Messeroffski
"Chipski"
"Cat High, love it or leave it."

MOST LIKELY TO: Leave it and still love it
LOYAL TO: His school and country and his teammates
PERSONAL CAMPAIGN: Support for CH athletics
PET PEEVES: being called a jock
OFTEN HEARD EXCLAIMING: "A jock is an athletic supporter."
DESTINY: To drive American cars
IDEA OF A GOOD TIME ON A SATURDAY NIGHT: Drive-in, dinner, the view from on top of Hartz Mountain, and Millicent McWhiskers
OFTEN SEEN: Saturday nights, driving Mr. Klinger's convertible

Fun lover . . . I need an extension . . . I need some sleep . . . I need some M&Ms . . . nice guy with secrets . . . double dates

ACTIVITIES: Hoopers 2,3,4; Band 4; Football 2,3,4; RATC 2,3,4; Rag Tag 2,3; Make Out Club 3,4; Hoods & Chassis 2,3,4

Mira Nightingale
"Pet"

"An apple a day keeps the bad marks away."

AMBITION: To stay in school forever
FAVORITE MOVIE: "To Sir, With Love"
MOST LIKELY TO: Win a good citizenship merit badge
FAVORITE MAGAZINE: Highlights
OFTEN HEARD SAYING: "Can I help you with that, Miss Maps?"
CLASS REP: Tattle Tailingale

Always clapping erasers . . . kisses lots of tail . . . likes staying after class . . . doesn't know what to do after 3:00 . . . T.G.I.M. . . . you know what would be really neat? . . . should I turn off the lights, Miss Mouseberger?

ACTIVITIES: Teacher's Aide 1,2,3,4; Lemon Aide 3,4; Gator Aide 3,4; First Aide 4; Band Aide 3,4

Annemarie Mousehaus
"Annie-kins"

"There's more to life than laughter and fun. I can't think of what it is offhand, but it's there."

SECRET PASSION: Kahlua and cream in a bowl
CAN BE FOUND: Watching old Cat Hepburn films
MOST LIKELY TO: Own a Betamanx
FAVORITE MOVIE: "Bringing Up Baby"
PET PEEVE: Popcorn stuck in her claws

Friends with Milly and Holly . . . the four-thirty movie! . . . the eight o'clock movie . . . the late show . . . french-fried mouse-skins and soda

ACTIVITIES: Field-mouse Hockey 3,4; Prom Refreshment Committee 3,4

BEST CITIZEN

Agatha Nosely
"Aggie Knows"

"To tell the truth, the whole truth, and . . ."

ROLE MODELS: Rona Barrett, Hedda Hopper, Louella Parsons
OFTEN HEARD SAYING: "If any of you become famous, my notes will be worth millions."
AMBITION: To be nationally syndicatted
FAVORITE SONG: "I Heard It Through the Grapevine"
FAVORITE T.V. SHOW: "Truth or Consequences"
SUSPECTED OF: The photo caper at the Yearbook office (all embarrassing negatives stolen)

Central Intelligence Agency . . . the Ear of Paw Paw . . . darling, you're really better off not knowing . . . carried a notebook to prom night . . . tipped off . . . I got it from a reliable source . . . but I never divulge my sources . . . I need a typewriter—*quick*!

ACTIVITIES: Chit Chat 1, Editor; Tabby Tatler 2; Catty Corner 3; "Aggie Knows" column, The Scratching Post 4; C.H.I.A. 1,2,3,4

Trixie Nixon
"Moxie"

"Cats who never get carried away should be."

WE'LL REMEMBER: Cheers at the Catpitol—give me a U, gimme an S, gimme an A
FAVORITE BOOK: "The Sound and The Furry"
FAVORITE AUTHOR: Marcel Purroust
DEBATE STANCE: Resolved—Garfield, Role Model or Anti-Hero
PET PEEVE: Garfield
LEGACY: The Nixon Tapes—Cats Domino, ZZ Topcat, James Tailer—what a party tape

Save me a seat . . . dance parties at Trixie's . . . wow . . . all this and brains too . . . purrky . . . catalyst

ACTIVITIES: Rise and Shiners 3,4; Pep Cats 2,3,4; Key Ticklers 4; Pro and Conners 2,3,4; Student Council Treasurer 4; Pussycats 2,3,4

Gill~ It was great having you in biology this spring— I remember the fetal mice.

Trixie

Gill sweetheart, you really don't have to be embarrassed about you-know-what 'cause I'll never tell you-know-who. Ssshhh! — Aggie
(The Nose KNOWS!)

MOST CATHLETIC

Catrine O'Ninetails
"Cat"

"Thoughts are the shadows of our feelings, always darker, emptier, simpler."—Nietzche

AMBITION: To marry into heavy metal
ROLE MODEL: Bianca Jaguar
OFTEN HEARD SAYING: "A hard cat is good to find"
FAVORITE SONG: "Hurts So Good"
BIGGEST DISAPPOINTMENT: Finding out that John Cougar's name is John Mellencamp
PET PEEVE: Wimps
FAMOUS FOR: Fur-for-alls at the O'Ninetails'

Three-inch nails . . . some cats aren't meant to be domesticated . . . biggest collar collection in the school . . . cigarette holder with studs . . . who's sorry now?

ACTIVITIES: Domino Trix 2,3,4; Heavy Metal Shop 4; 4th Base Anonymouse 3,4

It was great clawing you! Catrine

Tiger O'Malley
"The Big O"

"Let's win this one for the kipper!"

AMBITION: To be tight end for the Atlanta Falcons
OFTEN HEARD SAYING: "You can't hide when you're out on the football field."
PET PEEVE: Bad girls
FAVORITE SONG: "Bad Girls"
FAVORITE OCCUPATION: Dating bad girls on the sly
FAVORITE BOOK: "The Story of O"
FAVORITE MOVIE: "Zero for Conduct"
LEAST FAVORITE MOVIE: "Altered States"
NEVER SEEN WITHOUT: Cindy Tab or Sophie McMeow or Catrine O'Ninetails or . . .
REPUTATION: *The* cat who swallowed the canary

The winning season . . . how many falls before your mind gets soggy? . . . only 3 and already on life number 7 . . . lady killer . . . a real Tom's Tom . . . loves being called an animal

ACTIVITIES: Baseball 2,3,4; Football 2,3,4; Paw Twisting Club 0,1,2,3,4

Priscilla Pawsoff
"Prissy"

"This above all, to thine own self be true."

AMBITION: To marry a CPA
MOST LIKELY TO: Discover sex in college
FAVORITE MOVIE: "Snow White"
FAVORITE T.V. SHOW: "The Untouchables"
FAVORITE PHRASE: "Let's just be friends."
FAVORITE SONG: "Anticipation"
PET PEEVE: Toms who pet on the first date
OFTEN HEARD SAYING: "We've only known each other three years!"

Home by eight or else no date . . . frigid nose . . . mission impossible . . . no

ACTIVITIES: Home Economics 3,4; Cherry Jubilee Committee 1,2,3,4

Paloma Pawsano
"Picatso"

"Art isn't something you immediately understand."

ROLE MODEL: Jackson Pawlick
AMBITION: To starve in a garret
OFTEN HEARD SAYING: "Absinthe makes the heart grow fonder and the paws linger longer."
FAVORITE MEWSIC: "Pictures at an Exhibition"
PET PEEVE: Cretins who boast they know nothing about art but know what they like
GREATEST ARTISTIC INVENTION: Pawtailism

Paloma goes punk with pink whiskers . . . cray-paws . . . it's *Christo*, not Crisco . . . Joan Crawfish's cubist mice . . . even my parents don't understand me! . . . it offends my sensibilities . . . ars longa, vita brevis . . . the mouseholes in the principal's office

ACTIVITIES: Paw Paw Dada 3,4; Tasteful Palettes 2,3,4; Mouse of the Month Calendar 3,4; Drama Club Set Design 2,3,4; Pawtograph Club 1,2,3,4

MOST CHASTE

Kirk Quasar
"Spock"

"Space: the final frontier"

AMBITION: To be the first cat in space
MOST LIKELY TO: Be the first cat to drown in the Milky Way
OFTEN HEARD SAYING: "Beam me up, Scottie"
FAVORITE SONG: "The Star Trek Theme"
FAVORITE ACTRESS: Lieutenant Uhura
WE'LL ALWAYS REMEMBER: The Klingon Punch
BEST FRIEND: *Not* Stuart Ratatat

Captain, the engines . . . home by six every night for the reruns . . . what are wookies? . . . cardboard spaceship in his backyard . . . did you get a good look at the control panel?

ACTIVITIES: Junior NASA 3,4; Shop 4

Sue Purr
"Soup," "Sissy"

"Keep a fair-sized cemetery in your backyard, to bury the faults of your friends."

AMBITION: To be like Florence Nightingale
DESTINY: To be like Florence Henderson
MOST LIKELY TO: Be Den Mother to a Kitty Scout troop
FAVORITE TV SHOW: Veterinarian Hospital
OFTEN HEARD SAYING: "You guys have really got yourselves in a fix this time."
LAST GOOD DEED: Nursed a church mouse back to health

Candy-striper . . . meek . . . never been licked . . . nice to a fault . . . let me get out of your way . . . oh dear . . . wacko ward volunteer . . . where is everybody? . . . don't pick at that . . . the great Band-Aid Caper

ACTIVITIES: Health Club 1,2,3,4; Prom Clean Up Committee 2,3,4; First Aid Corps 2,3,4; Rummage Sale Boosterette 2,3,4

MOST INTERPLANETARY

MOST ENTERTAINING

Stuart Ratatat
"Stuey," "Stu," "Stoobie Doobie Do"
"You don't have to be a banana to be a still-life."

ROLE MODEL: Alfurred E. Newman
AMBITION: To revive vaudeville
NEVER SEEN WITHOUT: His Sleep Center Volunteer badge
OFTEN HEARD SAYING: "That stuff always makes me feel weird"
CLAIM TO FAME: The Siamese Fire Drill
OFTEN HEARD: Without opening his mouth
BEST FRIEND: Kirk Quasar
MOST LIKELY TO: Become a lounge singer
WILL BE REMEMBERED FOR: Graduating

Say it, don't spray it . . . O.D'd on No Doz . . . what me worry? . . . bow ties, white socks and black sneakers . . . knows the real lyrics to "Louie Louie" . . . bowling at Jane's without pins or a ball . . . absent in mind but there in spirit . . . like a Scrabble game without the vowels . . . the twilight zone . . . in loco parentis . . . knock knock? Stu's there.

ACTIVITIES: Emcee of Talent Night 4,5; Junior Stunt Night Emcee 3

Mike Redo
REDO REDO *"Mike Did-it"* REDO REDO!!
"If life is a bowl of herring, how come I only get the bones?"

AMBITION: To graduate before turning 30
MOST LIKELY TO: Greet you with a buzzer in his paw
FAVORITE MOVIE: "Catty Shack"
FAVORITE BOOK: ???
LAST BOOK READ: "Mad's Snappy Answers to Stupid Questions"
FAVORITE SUBJECT: Humor—at someone else's expense
OFTEN HEARD SAYING: "Can I be you?"

Eight year plan . . . just kidding . . . ketchup is too a vegetable . . . pleased to greet you . . . there's laughter whenever he's around . . . dynamite in the kitty litter . . . principal's office is his second home . . . you got your sheet together? . . . hairballs at ten paces . . . do unto others what you think is really funny . . . whose homework am I copying?

ACTIVITIES: Anglers 4; Key to the Principal's Office Club Founder 4; Squirt Gun Club 3,4; Fake Blood Donor 3; Rubber Chicken Booster 3,4; Fun Raiser Chaircat 4

You're cool but I'm cooler

Ratzy Rizzo
"Splash," "Captain Q"

"I can resist everything but temptation."

AMBITION: To shoot the Pipeline
LOVES: Big waves
PET PEEVE: Snow
FAVORITE MOVIE: "Endless Summer"
FAVORITE SONG: "Surfin' Safari"
OFTEN HEARD SAYING: "Keep your nip, I'm high on lives."
CLAIM TO FAME: Picture next to "hedonism" in dictionary
WE'LL REMEMBER: Fight with 'rents about having to join RATC

Surfs anything that moves, including Sally . . . surfin' for the U.S. in "Apocalypse Meow" . . . hang eight . . . loves piña clawadas . . . let's make waves!

ACTIVITIES: President, Talent Club 1; RATC 3,4; Meowlers 4; Dark Shades Society 2,4

Gill—Don't go liberal on me, ok? CFES III

Christofurr Fenwick Eggenliver Sandwich III
"Wick"

"If I owned Texas and Hell, I'd rent out Texas and live in Hell."—General Sheridan

AMBITION: To develop our national parks
DESTINY: To play the Fish Market
WILL MAKE 1ST MILLION: In Tuna Futures
OFTEN HEARD SAYING: "I should have gone to St. Paws."
PET PEEVES: Long-hairs
STUCK ON: Trixie Nixon

Morris was just kidding . . . the right element . . . Catillacs for all . . . we don't do that sort of thing . . . kill them all, let God sort them out . . . nothing like an endangered species—for breakfast

ACTIVITIES: Chaircat of Cats Against Wild-life 4; Flag Raisers 3,4

Jig Sawyer
"Mr. Fixit"

"I'll build a stairway to Paradise, with a new step every day."

FAVORITE SONG: "If I Had a Hammer"
FAVORITE ALBUM: "If I Were a Carpenter"
ALWAYS SEEN WITH: His paw in his mouth
PET PEEVE: Pet doors
OFTEN HEARD SAYING: "OWWWWWWW!"
FINEST ACCOMPLISHMENT: Constructed the first Mouse Motel (the mice check in, but they don't check out)

I am not a tool . . . built his own stereo . . . still trying to perfect the mousetrap . . . designs for the Stairway to Heaven . . . a throbbing paw

ACTIVITIES: Hoopers 3,4; RATC 2,3,4; Shop 1,2,3,4; President of the Draftsman Club 3,4

Edna Smelts
"Later"

"Don't walk in front of me, I may claw your leg. Don't walk behind me, you know why. Walk beside me, and just hold your nose."

AMBITION: To attend a party where others remain congregated
OFTEN HEARD SAYING: "That's a great cologne—can I borrow it? Now?"
FAVORITE PERFUME: Ralston
FAVORITE FOOD: Pickled herring
PET PEEVE: Hygiene class
HAS NEVER: Discover cedar chips

Not cut off without a scent . . . the nose knows . . . where did everybody go? . . . hope for the hopeless . . . wait up!

ACTIVITIES: Fish-Cleaning Team 3,4

Waylon Squeeks
"Wail"

"I went to the levy but the levy was dry."

AMBITION: To sing with Tabby Wynette
WILL PROBABLY END UP: Collecting pawtographs outside the Grand Ole Opry
FAVORITE SINGER: Johnny Catsh
FAVORITE SONG: "Thank God I'm a Country Cat"
OFTEN HEARD SAYING: "Jesus was a Nashville cat"
PET PEEVE: Heavy-metal devil-worshippers
STUCK ON: Cindy Tab

The ultimate bandana . . . my daddy worked on someone else's farm . . . summers by the old fishing hole . . . does a mean two-step double time . . . have y'all heard the latest Dolly Pawton record?

ACTIVITIES: Cats For Steel Guitar Strings 3,4; Chorus 1,2,3,4

Phyllis Snippitt
"Pinky"

"It's not *what* you say or do, it's how you *look* when you say it."

ROLE MODEL: Victoria Principaw
AMBITION: To be a Cosmo girl
DESTINY: To be a cosmonaut
FAVORITE SONG: "I've Got the Look You Want to Know Better"
OFTEN HEARD SAYING: "He's a ten"
PET PEEVE: Modesty
STUCK ON: Morris
WILL SETTLE FOR: Ezekiel Zooaster

Where's my make-up? . . . always in the bathroom . . . lifetime subscription to Cattymoiselle . . . P.T. . . . 27 shades of claw polish . . . beat it, buster . . . cheerleading is harder than it looks . . . I don't give out many tens

ACTIVITIES: Glamour Pusses 1,2,3,4; Pussycats 2,3; Astral Cats 2,3,4; Band 3,4

Nick Sturgeon
"Shar," "Nick the Knife," "Lucky"
"Live fast, die young, leave a nice corpse."

SPOTTED: Selling the Principal symphony tickets

LAST SEEN: Being interrogated for symphony ticket forgery

OFTEN HEARD SAYING: "You wanna make a bet?" "I'll give you good odds." "The House sticks."

FAVORITE MOVIE: "The Sting"

PROBABLE DESTINATION: Catlantic City

FAVORITE NUMBER: 21

NEVER WITHOUT: A fresh deck

STUCK ON: 17

Wheeling and dealing . . . with interest . . . anything for a buck . . . chips ahoy! . . . pool shark—but not the swimming kind . . . pick a card, any card

ACTIVITIES: Junketeers 1,2,3,4; Debate Team 1,2,3; Young Republicats 2,3

Cindy Tab
"Gidget"
"It's really bad luck to be behind at the end of the game."

AMBITION: To pledge the best college sorority

FAVORITE MEMORY OF CAT HIGH: Oh my God, being named Homecoming Queen

LOVES: Bon bons and pom poms

ALWAYS HEARD SAYING: "Gimme a C, gimme an A, Gimme a T."

TAB LOGIC: We should stay, 'cause otherwise we'll have to go.

FAVORITE T.V. SHOW: Monday Night Football (with Tiger)

LEAST FAVORITE T.V. SHOW: Monday Night Football (without Tiger)

FAVORITE OPERA: General Hospital

LAST BOOK READ: Wuthering Heights, Cliff Notes

Free meals for her friends at the Silver Tab . . . gabby but cute . . . c'mon gang a little more team spirit . . . strict parents . . . Miss Popularity . . . not tonight, I'm training

ACTIVITIES: Majorettes 2,3,4; Pep Club President 4; Astral Cats 2,3,4; Band 2,3; Pussycats 1,2,3,4; Homecoming Queen 4

Luv ya♥
Cindy

Bill—
Sorry you lost the football
pool. It was strange that
I won.
Nick

G-
I don't know
what to say
- C

Cheryl Tigres
"Meryl," "Tigger"

"Fasten your seat belts, everyone. It's going to be a bumpy night."—Bette Davis

OFTEN HEARD SAYING: "Talk to me in a stage whisper."
AMBITION: To play the lead in "Cats"
FAVORITE ACTRESS: Catrine Deneuve
FAVORITE ACTOR: Robert Redfurred
SECRETLY IN LOVE WITH: T.S. Alleycat
LOVES: Her leading men
HATES: Being upstaged
PET PEEVE: Directors
LIFE'S ACCOMPLISHMENT: Finishing Herman Hisse's "Demian"

Broadway bound . . . gets hot under the stagelights . . . the green room . . . little tigress . . . flirts in her sleep . . . best seat in the house . . . one more bow-WOW!

ACTIVITIES: Drama Club 2,3,4; Band, First Kazooist 4; Homecoming Runner-Up 4

Canardly Telwat
"Skitz"

"One's real life is so often the life that one does not lead."—Oscar Wilde

ROLE MODEL: Sybil
FAVORITE SONGS: "Night and Day," "Ebony and Ivory"
FAVORITE BOOK: "Drawing on the White Side of the Brain"
FAVORITE FILM: "The Three Faces of Eve"
FUTURE: Undecided

Topcat . . . on his way to Ratgers . . . daddy was, well, you know . . . spats for cats . . . ambiguity is my stock-in-trade . . . off and on . . . now and then . . . up and down . . . over and out

ACTIVITIES: Corvette Club 3,4; Mixed Chorus 2,3,4

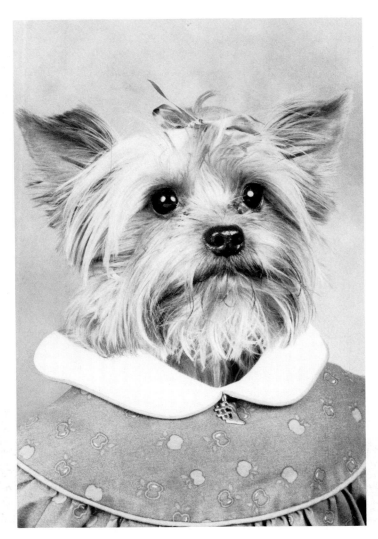

Felicia Faye Tirebiter
"Fido"

"I didn't ask to be bused to Cat High.
My parents didn't even vote for
President Johnson."

AMBITION: To date Benji just *once*

OFTEN HEARD BARKING: "Separate but equal . . . with a slight difference, perhaps."

ALSO HEARD BARKING: "Yes, I do find that word offensive. It's one thing to be called that by another female canine within my own kennel in my home community. And I staunchly reserve the right to refer to myself as such. But Prissy Pawsoff and Eva Feleinberg had better call me Felicia Faye unless they want to see my brother Butch in a dark alley on the way home from school."

WILL BE REMEMBERED FOR: A bark worse than her bite . . . but she barked a lot.

Some of my best friends are cats . . . bow wow wow . . . no good in the litter box . . . arf . . . oh, Finn!

ACTIVITIES: Committee on Interspecies Relations 2,3,4; Pussycats 3; Medically Excused From Phys. Ed. 1,2,3; Track Team 4; Whisker Lickers 2,3,4; Language Club 4

Saki Tumi
"Drowsy"

"It is better to sleep on things beforehand than to lie awake about them afterward."

ROLE MODEL: Sleeping Beauty
AMBITION: To be a mattress tester
MOST LIKELY TO: Sleep in
IDEA OF A GOOD TIME ON A SATURDAY NIGHT: Catnapping
FAVORITE MUSIC: White noise
FAVORITE BOOK: "Dreams, Reflections and Memories," by Cat Gut Jung

Wake me when it's over . . . out of it . . . good night in the morning . . . huh? . . . narcolepsy is not a drug enforcement agency

ACTIVITIES: Rip Van Winkle Club 1,2,3,4

MOST NAPS

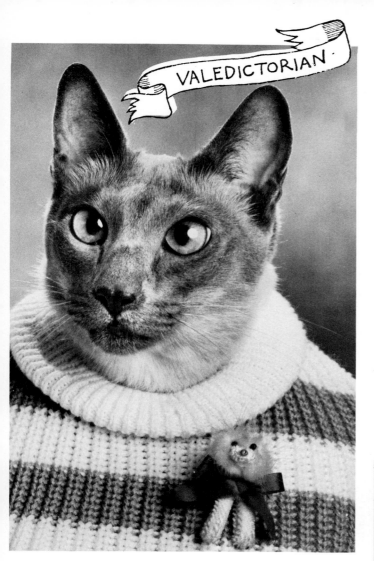

VALEDICTORIAN

Pawpurr Van Purr Purr
"Officer"

"The reason of the strongest is always the best."—La Fontaine

AMBITION: To make the world safe for democracy
MOST LIKELY TO: Tell it to the marines
PET PEEVE: Fraidy cats, copy cats, nipping cats
FAVORITE MOVIE: "Billie Jack"
OFTEN HEARD SAYING: "Hut two, three, four"

Sound body, sound mind . . . stand up straight . . . straight A's . . . straight arrow . . . hates vegetables . . . better dead than red . . . I don't see you saluting

ACTIVITIES: National Meowit Scholar 4; Vigilante Committee 2,3; Chief Pudknocker 4; Hoopers 3,4

Fly Straight. Pawpurr

Lulu Twitchfit
"Miss Know-it-all"

"A cat without knowledge is like a rat without a tail."

ROLE MODEL: Mr. Wizard
WILL BE REMEMBERED FOR: A mind like a mousetrap
MOST LIKELY TO: Study for the exam
FAVORITE MOVIE: "Brainstorm"
OFTEN HEARD SAYING: "It's no secret that the Siamese are a better breed."
BIGGEST TRAUMA: A B+ on her Catechism Exam

Miss Maps, I think you'll find Bélize is in Central America . . . all work and no play . . . I beg to differ . . . the eyes have it . . . ignorance is no excuse

ACTIVITIES: Honor Society 1,2,3,4; Meowlers 3,4; Oracle of Delphi Club 1,2,3,4; Siamese Society 1,2,3,4

Chester Winchester
"Chess"

"A mind is a terrible thing to waste."

AMBITION: To be chairman of the board
DESTINY: A checkered career
FAVORITE BOOK: "The Red and the Black"
SEX REP: Stale mate
OFTEN HEARD SAYING: "Paw to king's knight two."

Mr. Versatile . . . Harvard bound . . . walks old ladies across the street . . . is there some way I can help you? . . . j'adoute . . . potzer . . . rapid transit

ACTIVITIES: Chess Team 1,2,3,4; Tennis Captain 4; Pro and Conners 2,3,4

Felicity Von Furstenbreed
"Felicity"

"What becomes a legend most?"

AMBITION: To own the world's most expensive fur coat
FAVORITE MOVIE: "How to Marry a Millionaire"
HUSBAND FROM HISTORY: Louis Cat-orze
OFTEN HEARD SAYING: "Give me one in every color"
SECRET WISH: To spend a week in the Canary Islands with Christofurr eggenliver Sandwich III
FAVORITE COLOR: Himalayan White
WE'LL REMEMBER: Her purrloined plan to wed Abdul

In heaven an angel is nobody in particular . . . cream and caviar . . . a mouse is a present you give yourself . . . generous to a fault

ACTIVITIES: Fashion editor for the Scratching Post 2,3,4; Culture Club 3,4

Go from it!
—"Kattya"

Teresa Yikes
"Yessiree"

"Just because you're going through adolescence doesn't mean you have to act like one."

ROLE MODEL: Pollyanna
AMBITION: To bring new meaning to the word "square"
MOST LIKELY TO: Be shocked by Marie Osmond
FAVORITE DIRECTOR: Walt Disney
FAVORITE MOVIE: "Bambi"
OFTEN HEARD SAYING: "Popularity isn't everything. At least I've got my self-respect."
EVEN MORE OFTEN HEARD SAYING: "Will that be on the exam?"

Hormonal control . . . washes hands a lot . . . bathing suit has a skirt . . . is the "G spot" a clean movie? . . . sleeps with arms above the covers . . . what does Berkeley do that makes him so unstable? . . . well, o.k., I'll let you kiss my elbow . . . alcohol is for cleaning wounds

ACTIVITIES: Do Be Club 1,2; Don't Be Club 3,4; Stage Kissers 1,2,3,4; Slap in the Face Club 1,2,3,4; Future Shock 1,2,3,4

Kattja Witdagütz
"Kattya"

"A good thing is the encouragement of a friend."—Homer

IN HER OWN COUNTRY: Ludefisk Fishing Queen
AMBITION: To be Peer Gynt's sweetie
FAVORITE COMPOSER: Lawrence Welk
OFTEN HEARD SAYING: "How do you say in your language?"
OVERHEARD SAYING: Look Paw, no Hans
WE'LL REMEMBER: Her folks dancing

Let's have a polka party . . . would you mind very much to help me, please? . . . a sweet kid, but . . . wears skis to bed . . . vat else? . . . oofda . . . knows all the Ole and Lena jokes

ACTIVITIES: Exchange Student Seminar Spokescat 4; Polka Dot Club 4

She probably just saw José in his swim trunks!
—R.R.

Yin Yung

"The Inseparables"

Yang Yung

"I vant to be alone."—Greta Garbo

"Two heads are better than one"
—Siamese Proverb

AMBITION: To spend an evening alone
FAVORITE BOOK: "How to Be Your Own Best Friend"
FAVORITE SONG: "I Walk Alone"
FAVORITE MOVIE: "The Heart is a Lonely Hunter"
LOVES: Sleeping late, rock 'n' roll
LAST SEEN: Trying to make trouble
COLLEGE CHOICE: Ratcliffe

AMBITION: To maintain the connection
FAVORITE BOOK: "I'm O.K., You're O.K."
FAVORITE SONG: "Tea for Two"
FAVORITE MOVIE: "The Group"
LOVES: Getting up early, classical music
LAST SEEN: Trying to smooth things over
COLLEGE CHOICE: Yaowle

Tea for two . . . walking stereo . . . left hand doesn't know what the right's doing . . . I'll scratch your back if you'll scratch mine . . . two's company . . . I'm eating for two . . . double trouble . . . double features . . . a good coat is worth two thousand licks

ACTIVITIES: Tennis Doubles 2,3,4; Debating Team 1,2,3; Tag Team 1,2

GILL- CAN'T WAIT TILL YOU VISIT US AT RATCLIFFE! -YIN

GILL- CAN'T WAIT TILL YOU VISIT US AT YAOWLE! -YANG

Pyewacket Zoose
"Zug"

"Move over, Rover, and let Zuggy take over."

ROLE MODEL: Bella Catzug
AMBITION: To be the first she-cat to be elected to Paw Paw Kitty Council
MOST LIKELY TO: Be the first she-cat to be elected to Paw Paw Kitty Council
WE'LL REMEMBER: Burning her flea collar; leading ERA sit-in
FAVORITE BOOK: "The Feline Eunuch"
PET PEEVES: Right-to-Litters, being called "pussycat," phonies, snobs, pseudo-punks, neo-hippies, quasi-intellectuals, cats who think they are cool, cats who think they are tough, cats who think they are Cats

One cat, one vote . . . big hats . . . don't mess, Bozo . . . equal vittles for equal work . . . feisty

ACTIVITIES: Young Democats 1,2,3 President 4; Susan Sontag Society 1,2,3,4; Feline Farm Club Founder 2; Chaircat, Radish Committee 3,4; Mugwump Wumper 3,4;

Ezekiel Zooaster
"E.Z.," "Oysterizer"

"Love is the answer, but while you're looking for the answer, sex raises some pretty good questions."—Woody Allen

AMBITION: To poke all the Polka Dots
ROLE MODEL: Fritz the Cat
PET PEEVE: Girls who say no; girls who say yes but mean no
FAVORITE SONG: "Sexual Healing"
FAVORITE MOVIE: "In the Heat of the Night"
FAVORITE COME ON: "If I told you you had a good body, would you hold it against me?"
OFTEN HEARD SAYING: "Sure I'll respect you in the morning."

A puss in every port . . . Tom cat . . . you look just like your sister in this light . . . playing veterinarian . . . your sandbox or mine? . . . kisses and tells . . . would you look at those titmice! . . . so many cats, so little time

ACTIVITIES: Fieldmouse Hockey Spectator 2,3,4; Aphrodisiacs for Home Economics (sole member) 4

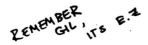

REMEMBER GIL, ITS E.Z

LAST WILL AND TESTAMENT

Zooey leaves his shades to Mr. Culpepper
Claws leaves many relieved teachers
Albert leaves with pomp and circumstance
Eins leaves his fleas to the circus
Zwie leaves in his brother's footsteps
Edsel leaves his socks to Mr. Furbanks
Rufus leaves his fastball to any junior
        that can take it
Finn leaves his leash to Catrine
Eva leaves her angst to Miss Mouseberger
Priscilla leaves her will power, and hopes
        that some underclass girl will want it
Chase leaves his opinion—on everything
Eugene leaves in a cloud of dust
Stanley leaves his address and phone number
Ratsy leaves his RATC uniform—gladly
Lulu leaves the study hall—reluctantly
Cindy leaves her pom poms to posterity
Waylon leaves for Juilliard
Sophie leaves her French accent to Joe
Joan leaves her mice models to Chef Le Pan
Cheryl exits stage left
Felicity leaves her cloth coat to Trixie Nixon
Mira leaves her bicycle seat to Mr. Humbert
Paloma leaves her self portrait to Tiger
Sue leaves an ℞ for the whole class
Mark leaves this ##&¢*$#%
        yearbook at the printer's
Jane leaves the complaint box yawning
Sushi leaves last year's watermelon espadrilles
Oscar leaves his senses
Edna leaves everything in her gym locker
Phyllis leaves a piece of her mind
Trixie leaves her tapes to Fleasia Grimm
Chaka leaves her little black book
        in a dressing room at the Maul
Aggie leaves her research to
        the Cat High archive
Pawline leaves her copy of "Miss Manners"
        to Slugger
Mary leaves on a broom
Saki leaves her pillow, reluctantly
Kattja leaves the country
Catrine leaves her handcuffs to Mike
Berkeley leaves his chemistry formulas
        taped to the boiler

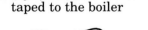

Chester leaves his queen in danger
Emma leaves 15 pounds to Stuart
Lars leaves his girlie pix in the enlarger
Melvin leaves his secret of success to Oedipuss
Canardly leaves his doubts
Pawpurr leaves us saluting
Collin leaves the Funny Button Club
        for the Funny Tie-Clip Club
Kunta leaves his family tree
Oedipuss leaves school to walk home
Albert leaves an existential question
        for the football team to ponder
Harmon leaves croonin'
Stanley leaves his hemostat to Berkeley
Kitty leaves everything;
        she'll get more later from daddy
Earnest can't spare anything
Spike leaves his eye patch
Hobart leaves port
Clawford leaves his principles to the Principal
Nelson leaves "The Writings of Nelson Fish"
Ezekiel leaves his Spanish Fly
        to the Entomology Department
Ntgabwe leaves his consonants
Catspurr leaves—thank god
Christofurr leaves it all in municipals
Baxter lets
T.S. leaves his candle burning
Beasly leaves on the rebound
Tiger leaves Cindy for Sophie
Jig leaves the Principal his old saws
Wally leaves unnoticed
Abdul leaves a new gym
Allen leaves this town full of losers
Sunshine leaves peacefully
Fred leaves his best to all
Nick leaves his nicknames
Kirk leaves his Vulcan handshake
Millicent leaves no clues
Annemarie leaves a ring around the bathtub
Pyewacket leaves in a huff
Rose leaves on the wings of angels
Holly leaves Paw Paw for Greenwich Village
Alison leaves for Saudi Arabia with guess who?
Yin and **Yang** leave through the same door
Teresa leaves intact
Mike keeps trying to leave
Felicia goes to the dogs

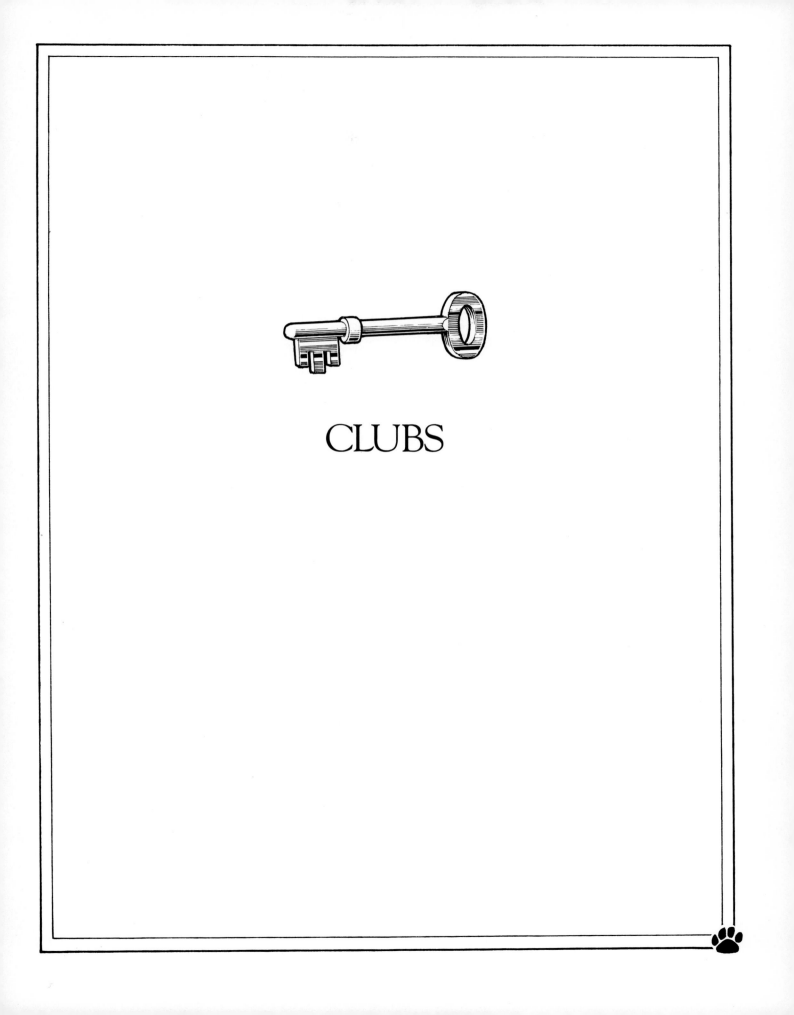

CLUBS

Give us a C!
Give us an A!
Give us a T!
What does that spell?!
We don't know!
Go, cats, go!

CHEERLEADERS:
THE PUSSYCATS

LEFT TO RIGHT:
Trixie Nixon;
Captain Sophie McMeow;
Kitty Tyler Katz

LEFT TO RIGHT:
Trixie Nixon;
Captain Sophie McMeow;
Cindy Tab

Honestly, we Pussycats can't tell you what fun it's been purr-leading this year. So we wrote a special song, just for the cats of Cat High. It's our small way of saying thanks for your support of our courageous cathletes this year.

Pussycats, Pussycats,
We love you—
Yes we do—
From our precious Pussycat eyes
To our cute little Pussycat toes.

And remember—*always* be true to your school.
Sophie McMeow
Captain

LEFT TO RIGHT:
Phyllis Snippitt;
Cindy Tab;
Trixie Nixon

CAT HIGH CHEER

Scratch 'em up, claw 'em up,
Throw 'em in the litter.
Let's show (other team) which team's fitter.
Suck 'em in, spit 'em out,
Give 'em a low blow.
Come on, Cat High, go, go, go!

LEFT TO RIGHT:
Kitty Tyler Katz; Sophie McMeow; Phyllis Snippitt
BACKGROUND (WINKING): Tiger O'Malley

THE CAT HIGH MARCHING BAND

When everybody showed up it went like this: Chatwick on triangle, Snippitt as flag bearer, Tab on drums, Fuzzerelli with the baton, Tigres on kazoo and Messeroffski waving his paws around. But when Phyllis and Cindy were busy with cheerleading, and Slugger and Chip were playing football, that left it up to Catspurr and Cheryl to play all the instruments. Fortunately all the instruments were a triangle, a drum and a kazoo. They sounded great.

LEFT TO RIGHT:
Triangle, Catspurr Chatwick;
Flag Bearer, Phyllis Snippitt;
Drums, Cindy Tab;
Baton, Eugene Fuzzerelli;
Kazoo, Cheryl Tigres;
Alternate Arm-waver, Chip Messeroffski

73

R.A.T.C.:
RESERVED ALLIANCE OF TOM CATS

Us cats, we is like General Sherman. Yes sir. Us cats of R.A.T.C., we hates war. But don't gets us wrong. If puss comes to shove, we is purrpared to scratch and claw for the Red, White and Blue. Yes sir. Us R.A.T.C. cats, we isn't scaredycats. We isn't afraid of no Commie gook bombs. No sir.

Us cats, we has got some wise words we lives by. Yes sir. They is fighting words. They goes like this:

"Do not needlessly endanger your lives until I give you the signal." General Eisenhowler—he said that.

"No matter how many cats fight, there always seem to be plenty of kittens." Abraham Lynxoln—he said that.

"We regrets that we has only nine lives we is able to give to our country." We R.A.T.C. cats—we says that all the time.
Ratsy Rizzo
Commander

LEFT TO RIGHT:
Lieutenant Jig Sawyer;
Corporal Chip Messeroffski;
Commander Ratsy Rizzo

Φ B K:
PHI BETTA KATTA
LEFT TO RIGHT:
"Book-wise" Lulu Twitchfit;
"Diligent" Catspurr Chatwick;
"Whiz Kid" Edsel Knudsen

What does Phi Betta Katta mean?

It means a great deal more than diligent, studious pursuits and the incidental attainment of a 3.9 gradepoint average. Phi Betta Kats help those cats less intellectually gifted than themselves through selfless school services such as tutoring members of the Little Dickens Motorcycle Club and representing CH on CATV's highschool game show "Quiz Cats." As the Society's chief grade-getter and Student Council president, Catspurr Chatwick, said at this spring's Brain Food Ceremony: "The Betta Kattas are not just a bunch of smartycat eggheads with high CQs analyzing highfalluting microchips and making snotty quips. We're committed."

Club vice president Edsel Knudsen concurred: "We're certainly not just a bunch of smartycat eggheads with high CQs analyzing highfalluting microchips and making snotty quips. We're committed."

THE DEBATING TEAM:
THE PROS-AND-CONNERS

It would be infinitely cheerier to report that the purrsuasive purrers purrformed purrfectly this year. But the immutable misfortunes of reality speak otherwise. The year in feline forensics bore a close resemblance to a year of feline follies—or in the words of Faculty Adviser Ratterwrong, "The Season of Unreason" for the Pros-and-Conners.

Appropriately, the subject of the year's first debate against Minniemousapolis High was "Resolved: Winning Isn't Everything, It Isn't Anything." We had the Mousers' case closed, until Ozzie Osgood ozoned on the rebuttal, and began humming "Love to Eat Them Mousies; Mousie's What I Love To Eat. . . ." Oz was plain nipped out, and we had to puss-and-boot him right off the team.

We figured our chances were pretty good against Catskill School for the Deaf and Dumb, with the subject, "Resolved: Fish Have No Civil Rights." But the whole ball of yarn came unraveled when Lars Endicatt, in attempting to demonstrate the affirmative, sautéed two dozen guppies before the dumbfounded audience, and the debate degenerated into a frenetic fish fry. We were DQ-ed, but well-fed.

Oh well—maybe we can't debate, but we sure can dance.
Trixie Nixon
Debate Team Captain

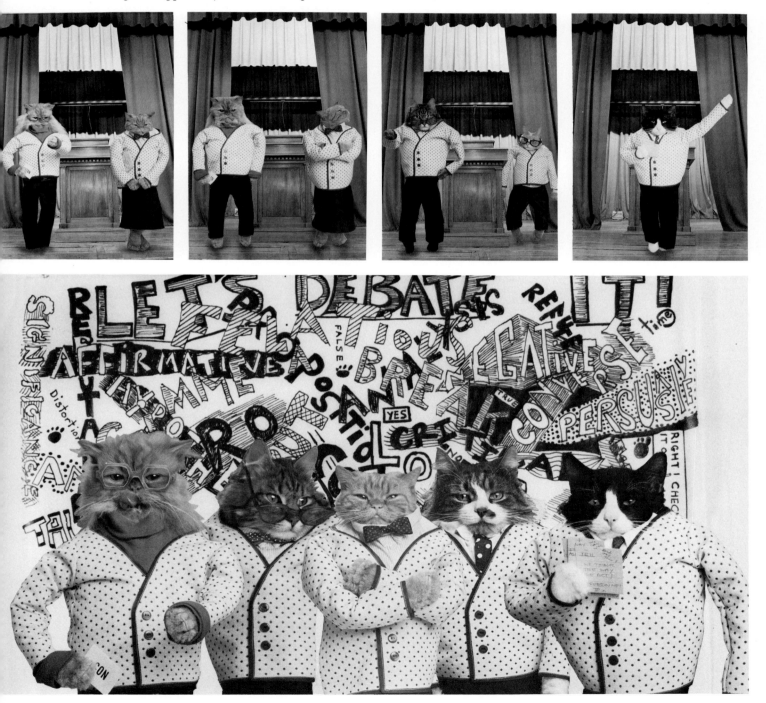

LEFT TO RIGHT: First Negative T.S. Alleycat; First Affirmative Harmon Cronin;
Second Negative Trixie Nixon; Alternate Lars Endicatt;
Second Affirmative Chester Winchester; Long Gone Oz Ozgood

LEFT TO RIGHT Das Kook Felicia Faye Tirebiter, ΓΘΘΚ Mark Mice,
La Chefesse Sophie McMeow, La Cookaracha José Jalapiña

Mon dieu! What a totally mucho superieur season! What a joie to learn how other cats vivre in countries around the world! So many moments magnifique! First, our dashing visitor from south of the frontière! José Jalapiña! That hombre Mexicain—pretty trés bien, eh?! Beaucoup de sex appeal and mucho macho! Quelle coup for the C.H. junior class! Ich du liebe, José! And the year's fiesta without equal—our nuit de food! Voulez-vous cooké avec moi ce soir?! Oui and Si! And cooké we did! So many choixes de menu to satisfy our bonnest appetitos! De Germany: Halibut Holstein (mmm!) and Filet von Fritz (trés mysterieux but trés tasty!)! De Spain: Chili con Catti (hold the tabasco!) and Pescado Tom Catto (fish with flair!)! Et from France: Purrée de Pommes au Chatin (it melts in your bouche!) and Mousse de Mouse (without tails—it's de rigueur!)! We were all trés stuffed! It was all so fantastique! But even though we have to say "Sayonara!", we will always remember the international flavor of Cat High!

Sophie McMeow
La Chefesse

ASTROMONY CLUB:
THE ASTRAL CATS

The moons are in Catpricorn right now, and so it's not a really good time to be writing, but the yearbook editor says it's "now or never," so we guess that means now.

The members of the Astromony Club—that's us, Cindy Tab and Phyllis Snippitt, learned a lot about stars this year. Like why Aquarian cats are kind of drippy and why Pisces guys just make your mouth water. We figured out that the reason Prissy Pawsoff got uptight and quit the club last semester was 'cause she's a Virgo and just doesn't know how to have a good time! We're both Leos so we just do what's fun and glamorous, because that's what the stars predict for us. We were even thinking of changing our club name to the Leo Club, but Adviser Mouseberger vetoed that idea saying, "We have to draw the lion somewhere."

Before we close we'd like to say thanx to Linda Goodcat for being so cosmic. Knowing the Little Dipper is nice and the Big Dipper is nicer, but show us Orion's Belt and tell us what's rising, and can we ever get excited!
Cindy Tab
Phyllis Snippit
Stars

CHESS CLUB:
THE CHECKBOARDERS

As coach and chaircat of the Chess Club, I want to congratulate the Checkerboarders for an undefeated mating season. The team made great checkmates and super stalemates—as well as sensational snackmates at the year-end "Love That Liver" Luncheon.

And there's more! This year, club captain Chester Winchester became the first Paw Paw pawn-pawer to achieve the honor of grand meowster. Ches earned his chevrons by demystifying the "Moscow magic" of Soviet grand meowster Boris Katsky, who made an unexpected visit to Cat High after his triumph at the Domesticated Animal Championship in nearby St. Paw.

Ches foiled the foreign feline by smoothly executing the adventurous cat-scratch gambit. Ches, pawing the black pieces, purrloined a half-dozen of the great Katsky's ivories before forcing the Russo-puss to resign on the 23rd move.

I wish all the Checker-boarders good luck in their future purrsuits—but especially Ches. For the name Ches has become virtually synonymous with chess at Cat High. Rook to Queen-4 . . . wow!
Mr. Bandersnatch
Coach

THE MATH CLUB:
MATHLETES

You know, life is like second-year algebra—just when you think you've got a problem solved, another problem shows up. You know what I mean?

Last year, the Mathletes' three-time all-stater, Bing Pawsby, hits graduation road. So long Bing, hello problem. Not to worry—we've got trig queen Alison Chow to fill the Binger's big shoes. So what happens? A.C. gets her writing paw caught in her Apple II disk drive. Busted paw. So long Alison, hello problem.

Except no problem is too tough for the catculators to handle. First, we dust off Dog High with a school record in the square-rooting. Then we punch St. Paw High's time clock in the state sine-off. Only a dismal dunking by Sylvester High—we really lunched out on the logarithms—spoiled a purrfect season for the smartycats.

The brains of our operation? None other than the Sultan of Sliderule, team captain Collin Devereaux. At the club's last meeting of the year, we voted Dev our MVP—Most Valuable Problem-Solver. The cat just devours derivatives.

Stanley Klinger
Secretary

LEFT TO RIGHT: Stanley "Rooter" Klinger;
Alison "Trig" Chow;
Collin "Calc" Devereaux

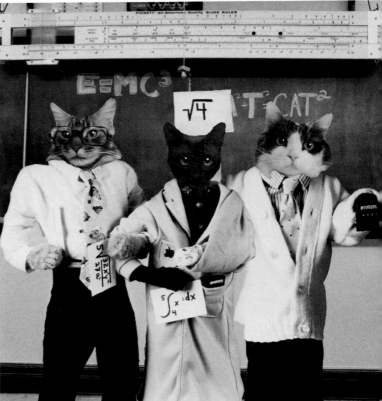

STUDENT COUNCIL

First, I'd like to thank all you cats who voted for me. It takes a tough smartycat to be president of Student Council. And I'm tough. But I'm honest. You can trust me.

I'd just like to say this about that: I'm purroud of my efforts on behalf of my fellow felines of Cat High. Now, you might be asking yourself: What did this cat do for Cat High this year? Well, I'm going to tell you. For one, I got Principal Grimm to rat-ify the new Dress Code. That was my idea. If it weren't for me, you'd have to leave those funky studded 3-in-1 collars at home. And the Morris Code—that was my idea, too. Now everybody at Cat High can act just as finicky as Morris—so long as it's not in class.

I know you're all wondering about my future. Well, I'm going to tell you. I'm grooming myself right now for a career as a Republicat. One day I'll run for Paw Paw Kitty Council. So be my friend, because remember—you can't fight Kitty Hall.

Catspurr Chatwick
President, Student Council

P.S. I apologize for having to schedule the Student Council officers' picture when Trixie Nixon, the Treasurer, was at cheerleading practice and Chip Messeroffski, the Secretary, was at a R.A.T.C. drill. But, it was the only time I could do it.

Student Government President Catspurr Chatwick
NOT PHOTOGRAPHED LEFT TO RIGHT:
Treasurer Trixie Nixon;
Secretary Chip Messeroffski

First Harley, Spike
"The Loner" Latigo

LEFT TO RIGHT:
Second Fuzzuki, Hopper Chopper;
First Fuzzuki, Eugene "Gino"
Fuzzerelli

MOTORCYCLE CLUB: THE HELL'S LITTLE DICKENS

Yo Spike, take this down will ya? It's fo da yeabook.

Da way I see it, da Cat High chapter of Hell's Little Dickens deserves a lot mo credit for the good deeds we done this year then we're gettin. All we keep hearing down here in Satan's Den is remarks like—and I quote: "We should disband Cat High's long-haired, chain-swinging bikers flaunting their impolite alley ways." Sue What's-her-face . . . yeh . . . Sue Purr said that. Who does she think she is, the queen of Sheba or something?

Nobody says nothin about us donated all our spare parts to charity. Did "The Scratching Post" ever even mention that we gave all the proceeds from the tickets for Evil Catnevil's death-defying leap over 14 litter boxes to Paw Paw Home fo Stray Cats? Just de other day me, Hopper Chopper and Spike lifted an ol' cat and carried her across a busy intersection to the other side. So what if she didn't want to go? So what if we also lifted her wallet? Why is that the only thing that everyone hears about? And how about the bake sale? No one can deny that those were the best brownies this side of Bogata. Hey, I take personal responsibility for the panty raid in the girls locker room. Nobody told me till afterward that you wasn't supposed to take the panties with the Pussies still in em. Remember, it was us that took the Principal hostage. Tell me the football team would have done that if he'd told *them* they didn't qualify as a varsity sport.

Later, cool cats . . . See ya on the road or under it.

Spike, just sign it Slugger, give it to Catrine. She'll deliver it, won't ya baby.

79

ART CLUB:
THE TASTEFUL PALETTES

The two of us got into some really cool stuff this year.

Our first project was the scenery for the musical "Cat on a Hot Tin Roof." We scratched out all those tacky backdrops from last year and gave the set design a new twist. Flattened tuna cans for the roof!!!!

Next, the school's Mouse-of-the-Month Calendar. That one turned into a pesky little pet project. . . . I MEAN, WHO ATE ALL THE MODELS???

Prank of the year—the mouse holes painted on the baseboards in Principal Grimm's office. And our one serious project . . . our 4-credit masterpiece . . . our Jackson Pawlick/Death to Paloma's Blue Period/Pawtailistic trip and a half: "The Pawprint-Covered, Tuna-Fish-Flecked, Paint-with-Your-Tail, Black-and-Yellowed Acrylic Canvas."

Let it be said that we sacrificed fur Art.
Joan Crawfish
Paloma Pawsano
Co-President

Joan Crawfish at work on "Principal Descending Staircase."

GLEE CLUB:
THE MEOWLERS

Yes, another year has been recorded in Meowler history—and recorded it was. That's right—as all you Cat Highers know, the hopeful harmonizers cut a record, and it's on sale right now at the Paw Paw Music and Novelty Shop. Just ask for "Songs to Lick Fur To."

But we're not here to sell records. We're here to give the Meowlers a rousing round of apaws for another fine year of croonin' and tunin'. The sevensome

took their act on the road, serenading the Semi-Rotary Club, the Paw Paw Order of Odd Felines, and the Alleycat Alliance.

Of course, the year's showstopper had to be the Meowlers' impromptu improvisation of "Do You Believe in Magic (We Don't)" at the Senior Class Party at Moonboy's Fish and Chips. Even Ol' Mooner himself tuned in on the last verse.

Credit for the Meowlers' musicalité magnifique goes to the boss basso, the leader of the litter, Professor ("Croonin'") Cronin. And, of course, the wondrous warblers won't be the same next year without graduating senior songsters like Glee Club president Sophie McMeow. But hey— that's show biz. The song must go on.
Phyllis Snippitt
First Soprano

*FRONT ROW: Tenor T.S. Alleycat; Second Alto Catspurr Chatwick;
First Soprano Phyllis Snippitt; Bass Harmon Cronin;
Second Soprano Sophie McMeow*
BACK ROW: Alto Ratsy Rizzo; Third Alto Lulu Twitchfit

And who could forget...

Our Junior Play

Romeow & Julicat

CAT ON A HOT TIN ROOF!

An original review.

Our Senior Play

"Cat On A Hot Tin Roof"
Cast

Maggie the Cat	Cheryl Tigres
Brick	Baxter Loveset
Harold "The Shingler"	Fred Fur
Chimney Sweep	Joan Crawfish
Big Daddy	Earnest Bootstraps
Fuller Brush Cat	Abdul Catdabra

"Romeow and Julicat"
Cast

Romeow	Charles de Chandon (Chip Messeroffski)
Julicat	Priscilla Pawsoff
Nurse	Eva Feleinberg
Friar Lawrence	Albert Cheshire
Lady Capulet	Cheryl Tigres
Mercutio	Collin Devereaux
Tybalt	T.S. Alleycat

Shakespeare said it and he was right, "All the world's a stage and all the cats merely players." The immortal Bard must have had our own drama society in mind when he penned those prophetic words. And we bet he would have raved over our highly poetic production of "Romeow and Julicat." As the junior play, this tragic tail of two young cats in heat certainly left the audience with wet whiskers. No one would have guessed that *total* chaos had broken out during dress rehearsal, when director Ouiounon threatened to replace Julicat (Prissy Pawsoff) during the torrid balcony scene because she would not "take direction." But, to quote the Bard once more, "The show must go on"— and it did: a triumph of art over Prissy-ness.

For our senior year we turned from classics to modern unrealism with an adapted version of "Cat On A Hot Tin Roof" written by Mike Redo in the lunchroom on a stack of napkins. The not inconsiderable talents of Cheryl Tigres in the lead role, Maggie the Cat, brought paws together and catcaphonous yowls and cat calls from the balcony. The critics, T.S. Alleycat and Paw Purr Van Purrpurr, may have ridiculed the radicalized production, but the audience just couldn't get enough of the bikini-clad Cheryl as she divided her attentions between the Fuller Brush Cat at the door and the Shingler on the roof.

To those who have kept us entertained these past 4 years, go out and break a hind leg on that big stage called nine-lives.

ACTIVITIES

HOM

Rastafurr and the Dreadwhiskers had their locks and licks together when they took the Homecoming stage and did their opening number: "Catnip: My Religion." The driving beat brought a full gymnasium to the dance floor shimmying, fruging, twisting and shouting to the furnetic mewsic. One cat spun on his head as the crowd watched him "break it."

Cindy Tab, the Homecoming Queen, summed up the event by saying: "You had to be there." We were!

Dear Class,

You know, these last six years have been great for me, and I'm sure they've been great for you too, because they sure have been great for me.

God, there's so much I'll remember about Cat High when I look back—even today. For instance Mr. Humbert's cute paws in gym class, or Principal Grimm's bobbed tail, or how about the whole football team? And I'll always remember the good times we shared at the spring festival and the good times we shared on Animal Day.

And how can I ever forget the day I was named Homecoming Queen? For me, it was the yeowler of the whole homecoming. Sure, we lost, but a higher score would have easily made the difference. All you Pussycats who weren't elected "Queen" shouldn't feel bad and take it as meaning you didn't win. I mean, good looks are only fur deep. And lots of girls did a lot better on the C.A.T.'s than me. There are probably other important things too—I just can't think of any.

Luv ya,
Cindy Tab

Paris In April

Cat Calloway and His Melodious Mousers set the tone for this year's prom, Paris in April, with tunes that sent seniors clawing up the gym floor like never before. The invitation called for "Black Collar Optional" attire, and that brought out some great new Tux "R" Us fashions, talk about cat fancies! But as beautiful as every feline was that night, Prom Queen Sophie McMeow stole the show, arriving in a gorgeous Catglama fur stole. The prom was not without its catastrophies: a salivating stream of streakers from Dog High brought pink to many faces. Mike Redo yanked the fire alarm for one last time during the slow dance "Catwalk to Heaven," making a noise so loud it sent couples scurrying from every dark recess of the gym, every broom closet, every empty classroom, and every bush. But trust ol' Berkeley Fumes to save the evening, spiking the punch with we dare not ask what. You've never seen such cat-dancing. All in all it truly was a catztravaganza to remember.

T.S. Alleycat and Phyllis Snippitt

Polly Dactyl and Lars Endicatt

Chester Winchester and Trixie Nixon

Eugene Tuzzerelli

Harmon Cronin

Eins Katzenjammer

Oscar Hiss

Tiger O'Malley and Pawline Madison

Zooey Furlinghetti and Cindy Tab

Rufus Cubs and Kitty Tyler Katz

Spike Latigo

Baxter Loveset

Harmon Cronin and Trixie Nixon

Phyllis Snippitt and Tiger O'Malley

Memories

"Patissier"—Stuart Ratatat

"Mlle. Follies Bergers"—Holly Mackerel

"Artiste"—Ezekiel Zooastor

Polly Dactyl and Hobart Lufter

Phyllis Snippitt and Baxter Loveset

Eugene Fuzzerelli and Sophie McMeow

Chester Winchester and Phyllis Snippitt

to Always

Trixie Nixon and Catspurr Chatwick

"Marie Antionette"—Priscilla Pawsoff

Louise Lyons and T.S. Alleycat

Remember

King Catspurr & Queen Sophie

Prom King and Queen Catspurr Chatwick and Sophie McMeow enjoy post-prom festivities at the Silver Tab (Cindy Tab's father's diner).

THE SENIOR·CLASS GOES TO WASHINGTON

Photography by Lars Endicatt and Mark Mice

There had been **ANTICIPATION** in the air for weeks. It was our big chance to escape Paw Paw for a while and step aboard our magic carpet to the Nation's Catpitol, Washington, D.C. So, when the moment finally arrived and the Tail Ways bus rolled up in front of the Gymnasium, we eagerly scratched our way into the best seats next to our bestest of friends.

Some of us thought it would be a 24-hour nonstop **door-to-door Snoozorama.** Were we ever wrong! First the RATC crew hogged the front row seats and made all the other cats salute them as they passed. Behind them sat Priscilla Pawsoff and Earnest Bootstraps. The two of them discussed the virtues of Virtue until we thought we'd throw up. The Little Dickens trio sat behind Priscilla, taunting her with vulgar wisecracks. Fortunately, the Diplocat crowd situated themselves in the center of the bus so they could appease all the catstituencies. After all, we were on a trip to the catbird seat of world politics.

That left a huge gap in the rear of the bus for the jocks and cheerleaders to fill with caterwauling. **The Red Eye crowd**—Berkeley Fumes, Zooey Furlinghetti, Chaka Khat, Paloma Pawsano, and Allen Mange—were nipping up a storm in the last two rows and teasing Eins Katzenjammer, who was listening to

GREAT PRANK

GUESS WHO☇

Off the bus with "The Merry Pranksters"!

Ratsy and Lars discover the self-timer.

his Sony Walkcat, by moving their lips but not saying anything. The rubber-chicken clique—Melvin Lick, Mike Redo, and Clawford MacLeash—spent their time trying to get a rise out of "Sleepy Puss" Saki Tumi. Tiger O'Malley shuttled between Sophie McMeow, Curiosity Kildecat, and old flame Kitty Tyler Katz, offering each a neck moussage.

Despite all the racket, T.S. Alleycat wrote several vignettes for his new play, "The Cattail Party." Chester Winchester, Alison Chow, and Abdul Catdabra discussed International Politics, while next to them the Siamese Twins argued over where they wanted to go to college. (Could it be Splitsville for Cat High's best-connected duo?) It was a happy crowd, full of most of the purrsonalities we'd come to know and love—or know and hate—over the past four years.

The big question was: could Cat High seniors create more trouble than on last year's trip to the planetarium? A tough act to follow, but Mrs. Withers, our chatperone, would soon see what kind of stuff we were made of.

We had hardly gotten into 10th gear when Chaka decided that she had to use the litter box and fast. The bus driver stopped and Chaka, Zooey **and** Allen got out. After about 15 minutes Mrs. Withers thought that maybe something was wrong. Boy was it ever! As she ran out to get them, the three of them came back giggling—**out-of-control!** Priscilla said we shouldn't let them back on, and it nearly came to a fight. Then Spike came up and said that if we weren't moving in two minutes he would drive the bus himself. There were no more mishaps—on the bus, anyway.

Washington, as a city, was great

although **I don't remember much** in terms of monuments. What I can say is that with two broken mattresses after only the first night, our real interests were not too political. Admittedly, Eins should not have been teaching the jitter-cat to Sushi Chew on the bed, but where else can you do flips and land softly? (Sushi claims she always landed on her feet.)

It was at this point (one broken mattress) that Tiger decided to play **spin the milk-bottle.** Even myself, the editor, could hardly keep cool when that bottle landed on Sophie. Too bad Earnest was sharing the room with us. **He burst in** as I was about to put my paws around Sophie (after having spent the evening with Priscilla, memorizing the D.C. Guidebook), and instead of a lot of fireworks, I quickly had to open the bottle and drink the milk so that he wouldn't catch on and snitch.

Senator, got a light?

You mean they just gave this all to you?   93

Gitty-up George!

Milly, Holly and Annemarie were entertaining Kirk, Zooey, Edsel and Allen (Allen?—yes, he and Holly were quite a pair that week) with the Kahlua-and-cream that Annemarie had snuck in. Emma Grouse, however, got really sick—it must have been all those trips to the Little Friskies buffet—and so another mattress was ruined.

Miss Withers was **disgusted and threatened** to suspend us all if we did not settle down—and fast. Spike and Claws were nowhere to be seen—they had found a group of kindred spirits and went off into the night.

"The best way to be understood is to say it loud!"
—Tabby Hoffman
(one of the Purina Seven)

No 21-gun salute?!

Finally, we all settled in for what little rest we could before a big day of sightseeing. The only one who got a full night's rest was Chase Betterborn, who konked out early from jet-lag. (Bus travel is not his style; he chartered a plane and met us at the hotel.)

The next few days, they tell me, were spent sightseeing, but I too had gotten sick and spent the rest of the trip in the hotel being nursed back to health by Kitty. I could tell you about her **curative powers,** but she's shy and we don't need to go into it.

Anyhow, I managed to recover just in time for the final celebration: Dinner at the famed Lion d'Or, where **Washington's Movers and Stretchers** gather for power lunches. Abdul was treating Alison, and bought her the Fish-of-the-Day special. Alison was so starry eyed she couldn't add up the check! Talk about Arabian Nights—I'm just dying to know where those two spent their evenings. Aggie says she plans a special column in The Scratching Post on just this **mysterious tidbit,** but she did fill me in on a lot of the action that I missed.

More memories to always remember.

The most embarrassing moment (at least for poor Mrs. Withers) was when **Melvin's rubber chicken** somehow jumped off the balcony of the Senate's visitors gallery, landing on the head of Michigan's very own Senator Pompuss. This was just as the Congress was voting on a bill to curb juvenile delinquency, and Melvin was almost hauled onto the floor as Exhibit A. Luckily, **confusion reigned** on the floor of the Senate, allowing us to beat a hasty retreat before being nabbed by the Catpitol police. It's nice to think that we made our own bit of history on our class trip to this most historical—or should I say **hysterical**—city.

To some, the most fun was the bus ride home.

SPORTS

A
BASEBALL
YARN

Just a couple of things I want to set straight about the team, because there've been a lot of rumors flying around. First off, we weren't the cats who clawed the covers off all the baseballs. Hey—there are better ways to get at a ball of yarn without resorting to vandalism. And second, we don't use nip to get up for the game. O.K., maybe a snort or two between innings—but that's it.

As for our season, I think the scores speak for themselves:

4–4 (spaced in the eighth; missed the team bus)

7–11 (liver slurpies for nine, to go)

3–3½ (who knows?)

9 (lives of a cat *and* innings in a ballgame)

Of course, we'd like to thank Abra Catdabra, Abdul's dad. for our new diamond. What a home-field advantage having an infield in the shape of Saudi Arabia! (Personal to Abdul: home plate does face east.)

"Zooey, you're supposed to run the bases the other way!"

FT TO RIGHT: Edsel Knudsen—out in left field; Eins "Shoestring" Katzenjammer—
ght field; Zooey "Bobbles" Furlinghetti—third base; Harmon "Hairball" Cronin—
tcher; T.S. "B.S." Alleycat—second base; Tiger "Bomb" O'Malley—captain, center
ld; Rufus "Groundhog" Cubs—shortstop; Spike "Let-it-go" Latigo—left field;
atspurr "Kingfish" Chatwick—first base; Baxter "The Scrapster" Loveset—catcher

"Joy in Mudville" by Mark Mice

IT TAKES GUTS TO PLAY TENNIS

TENNIS TEAM: THE RACKATS

When Coach Nobull made us read Rod Liver's book, *Cat on A Hot Clay Court*, at the start of the season, I think the whole team figured, "Oh, no—not another cat book." But now we sure love Liver. His last chapter—"It Takes Guts To Play Tennis"—was just the inspurration we needed to whip the Rin Tin Tennis-players from Dog High. As usual the boorish Bowsers showed total disregard for tennis eticat. Once again, they rounded up a mangey band of ASPCA rejects to parade around the court with PUNS (Pussies Use Nylon Strings) banners. (Actually, we use camel-gut, thanks to Abdul's dad.) They barked and growled at every line-call—a regular bunch of MacEnfidos. But we didn't let their animalistic antics get to us.

We closed out the match in style with Baxter Loveset's stunning upset of Goofy Gonzales. Too bad Baxy's heroic effort landed him in Paw Paw Veterinary with tennis elbow. But that just made for a great team party in the rest-and-rehab ward. Let me warn you, though—that intravenous catnip is pretty wacky stuff!

TRACK

Track and Field events are Felicia Faye Tirebiter's forte. Her years of chasing cars and jumping fences have kept her in top shape, and her only regret is that Track and Field has never been made an official Cat High sport. "Most cats just don't seem to like running any distance at all," says Felicia, "but I've always wanted to participate in Dog High's annual meat—if only to see their double-take when the Cat High team turns out to be a dog."
Felicia trains on a rigorous diet of high protein Alpo—sounds *really* yucky to us! She routinely clears the Cata-pole at 5 feet, beating the previous Cat High Jump record of 3 feet, 11 inches (set by Osci Springer 2 years ago.)

ALL STAR CAT HIGH PLAYERS

THE SEASON

CHS	34	Scent Vincent's	9
CHS	27	St. Paw	14
CHS	41	Turkey Tech	24
CHS	24	Ratskill	10
CHS	3	Dog High	42

LEFT TO RIGHT: Edsel Knudsen—loose end; Tiger O'Malley—captain, quarterback; Zooey Furlinghetti—eighthback; Eugene Fuzzerelli—laidback; Rufus Cubs—halfback
FOREGROUND: Albert Cheshire—tailback; Mark Mice—tight end

We dedicated our season to our retiring coach, Fred Ball Whiskers, who as every CH cat knows ended his career as the Ratters' Rasputin this year. Our goal was to win one for the Whiskers.

Actually we won four—and that's because the team was really cooking. We skewered the skunks of Scent Vincent's (their offense really stunk), pancaked the pussies of St. Paw High, goulashed the gobblers of Turkey Tech, and roasted the rodents of Ratskill School for the Deaf and Dumb. Only the bone-breaking bowsers of Dog High burst the bubble on a purrfect season.

Naturally we'd like to thank Abdul Catdabra's dad for providing us with our new uniforms. So what if the names on the backs of our jerseys were in Arabic?

CLOCKWISE FROM BOTTOM CENTER: Tiger O'Malley—captain, quarterback; Rufus Cubs—halfback; Mark Mice—tight end; Zooey Furlinghetti—eighthback; Albert Cheshire—tailback; Edsel Knudsen—loose end; Chip Messeroffski—center; Eins Katzenjammer—split end

THE SWIM TEAM: Aquaticat

José Jalapiña is my name,
Cat High's only swimmer, is my claim to fame.
I from Mexico where is mucho hot.
Think is joke? Well is *not*.
The weatherman say: Chili today, hot tamale!
Cats in water all day—is very jolly.
My best time in chicken-breast stroke,
10 yard record—only Dog's broke.
I faster against dogs than water rats,
I sure the fastest of all the cats.
You know I wish more cats like I,
Maybe we not lose and be disqualify.

FISHING TEAM: THE ANGLERS
CATCH AS CAT CAN

When we joined the Anglers four years ago as freshkittens, about the only thing we could catch was a cold. Now we're a reel bunch of afishionados, thanks to the oil-filled flyrods we got from Abdul Catdabra's dad. The team set school records in everything from smelts to tuna. But there were days this year when the fish just weren't biting—like this fall's Flounder Festival.

What a whale of a weird time! Wally Mackerel thought he had caught a ferocious flatfish on his first cast. So what does it turn out to be? José Jalapiña, training for the state Aquaticat Championships. Then Oedipuss Arbuckle reeled in some unidentified floating object that seemed pretty fishy— especially when Berkeley Fumes broke off a piece and smoked it. After that, the Fumes did a little floating of his own.

When it was all over, our Festival catch looked like a pile of thrift-shop rejects: two flea collars, a rusty whisker-trimmer, three Cats Domino 45s, and a prayer shawl from Eva Feleinberg's Bas Mitzvah.

Catch as cat can—that's the Angler motto. Usually we live by it. At the Festival, we cried by it.

LEFT TO RIGHT: Mark Mice—captain;
Wally Mackerel—fish scaler;
Berkeley Fumes—night crawler;
Oedipuss Arbuckle—bait boy;
Mike Redo—rubber worm monitor

ISLAND RULES
NO ALCOHOLIC BEVERAGE ALLOWED
FISHING FROM ANY PART OF ISLAND
OR BRIDGE PROHIBITED

DOG HIGH   24   CHS   DQ
ST PAW   17   CHS   DQ
MINNIEMOUSAPOLIS   41   CHS   DQ

LEFT TO RIGHT: José Jalapiña

MAPLE ISLE
Owned and maintained by
Village of Paw Paw

IF YOU CAN'T BEAT 'EM, EAT 'EM.

THE BASKETBALL TEAM

No guts, no glory: That's the motto of the Feline Five. And you just *know* we had to have our cat guts strung tight for the big game against Dog High. I mean, it wasn't like playing Mouse High, where we figured, "If you can't beat 'em, eat 'em." (We ate 'em.) Those dunking doggies were *awesome.*

The bowserballers had this cockapoo who could jump right out of the building— which he did, halfway through the second quarter. But with two seconds left, Beazly (the Blaze) Dweezle swiped the ball from the fumbling Fidos and executed an elegant half-gainer through the hoop for the winning swish. It took us just 20 minutes to get the Blaze untangled from the net.

A lot of people should be thanked for our success, but mostly Abdul Catdabra's dad, who bought us our new gym shoes. I mean, wasn't it great being the only hoopsters in Paw Paw with camel-hair sneakers?

LEFT TO RIGHT, BOTTOM ROW: Chip "Splinterbutt" Messeroffski —bench warmer;
Kunta "Dribble" Kitta—goal tender;
Beasly "The Blaze" Dweezle—right forward; Stretch
SECOND ROW: Pawpurr "Chevy" Van Purr Purr—right guard;
Jig "Jumpshot" Sawyer— captain, left guard
TOP OF THE HEAP: Rufus "Feed Me" Cubs—center forward

PUBLICATIONS

If Sophie M⁼ Meow married
Oscar Hiss she'd be
Sophie M⁼ Meow-Hiss ♡

The

SCRATCHING

Vol. XXXVI

POST

ALL THE MEWS

FIT TO PRINT

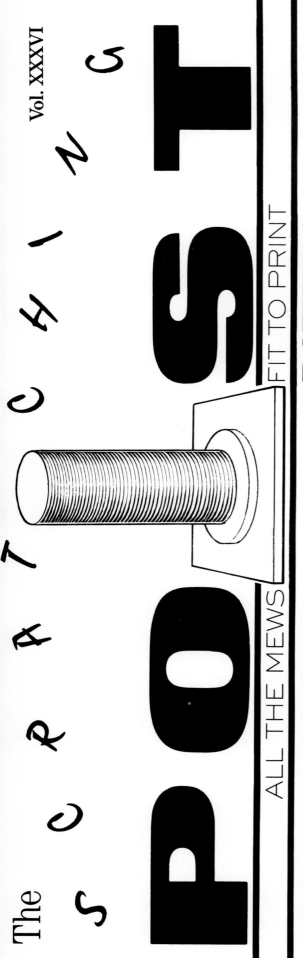

PROTESTERS PICKET MORRIS SPEECH

PAW PAW, Feb. 31—The arrival Friday of the Famed Finicky Feeder, TV's *Morris The Cat*™, inspired Cat High student demonstrators to air a broad array of grievances. CATV cameras on hand to cover Mr. The Cat's speech to the Paw Paw Republicats had more to cover than they could chew when 20 demonstrators with placards bearing signs reading "No Neuters," "Nay on Spay," "Free the Purina 7," "Remember Cattica," and "Morris Sold Out," blocked Mr. The Cat from delivering his speech, "How I Ate and Slept My Way to the Top."

"We tried like crazy to get someone or thing less controversial," said *Cherry Winetrout*, chaircat of the organization. Reportedly, their first choice was *E.T.*, but he did not return repeated phone calls to his home. *Sylvester*, the well-known TV star, declined the invitation because, he said, "I'm just a cartoon character." Other promi-

RATTERS BOW TO BOWSERS

Archrivals on and off the playing field, the Dog High Bowsers buried the bone and our fearless Cat High feline footballers 42 to 3 in the bi-annual cat and dog fight at Vince Lompawdi Field. The Ratters' home-field advantage and stylish scratch-and-claw play were simply not enough to provide the punch to powder those pooches.

The Bowsers dominated the game from the opening kick-off, with 3 consecutive touchdowns by tailback *Bobby Greyhound*, who penetrated all the holes in the Ratter's defense. On defense, the *Bulldog* brothers, *Otis* and *Bubba*, blocked, clogged and tripped up every attempt at a Cat High touchdown. "Add insult, injuries and missed opportunities to 40 penalties and it spells defeat," said retiring Cat High *Coach F. Ball Whiskers*,

"but if you ignore that, I think we did pretty well."

The penalties the Ratters incurred, an unheard-of 10 unsportsman-like conduct violations, came for hissing, spraying and raising their backs, ignited by *Adolph Shepard* calling the team "a bunch of pussies." Dog High's only penalty came in the third quarter when their mascot, the *Roving Fire Hydrant*, began mating with the Poodles' head cheerleader.

"We failed to bring home the Golden Milk Bowl," said *Coach Whiskers*. "It's been nailed to the floor at the Bowser Club for 132 years. Maybe someday it'll be installed in our cateteria."

[Cont. p. 4, col. 3]

ON THE INSIDE

AGGIE KNOWS AND TELLS ALL PG. 6

CURIOSITY KILLS STAR STUDENT

COPS NAB CAT HIGH NIPPERS

PAW PAW, Feb. 31—An anonymouse phone call to Paw Paw police put authorities on the tail of two Cat High students and a large shipment of Catalonian Catnip this past Wednesday.

The cat and mouse tactics led police to the Paw Paw Pier where 100 crates stamped TUNA in psychedelic lettering proved even fishier than expected. "The crates contained 40 kilos of Nipus Felinibus Sensinippa," **Captain Haggerty** of the Narcotics Squad said, "worth millions in the alley."

Felix dePauvrien, a junior, and treasurer of the Entrepreneurs Club, was held on $1,000 bail in the incident. The other cat's name will not be released until *Mr. and Mrs. Fumes* return from a trip.

Drug-related embarrassment is not new to Paw Paw. Two years ago, *Archimedes Liverschnapps* was awarded a Science Medal for a cure for cataracts which turned out to be wine-soaked "Paw Paw Purple," a locally-grown variety of the Catnip family.

BONES GRIMM TO RETIRE

Thelonius T.G. Bones Grimm IX, principal of Cat High for eight lives, announced in an emotional all-school assembly that he would lay down his paddle and his pen, and retire at the end of the school year.

"I want to leave the pitter-patter of young cats' paws and the hallowed sound of school sirens behind me and just veg out for a while. My wife and I are thinking of moving to Bermewda," the principal said. He joins *F. Ball Whiskers* as the second Cat High administrator to announce retirement this year.

Grimm will be succeeded by *Thackery Furbanks*, the vice principal. Grimm's innovations over his eight long lives at Cat High are as follows:

    I. The one-way stairs rule.
    II. All-day lunches.
    III. Edible hall passes.
    IV. The expanded Nap Room hours.
    V. The Morris Code.

STUDENT COUNCIL DEBATES MICE AND VICE

The Student Council met last week to vote on on the theme for this year's Senior Prom, changes in the lunch menu, and the newly created Mouse Patrol.

Unfortunately, the issues provoked considerable controversy, and the meeting was adjourned with several problems unresolved. "There was a split down the middle on the Prom question," announced Student Council President *Catspurr Chatwick*. *Abdul Catdabra* had a lot of cats behind him on the move to make it an 'Arabian Nights' theme; a lot of the guys were really psyched to go whole hog and hire belly-dancers." But a more conservative group maintained that "Paris in April" had been a great theme for the past ten years. "So why change now?" asked *Ernest Bootstraps*, president of the Young Republicats. "Besides which, we already have all the props and decorations."

Another argument raged on the Tuna-vs.-Liver question when the floor was opened on the Lunch Menu Resolution. After an impassioned speech by *Lars Endicatt* on "Liver—Can We Deliver?" and an equally stirring rebuttal from *Trixie Nixon*: "Never Too Tuna," the Council agreed that the issue was much too important to be decided hastily and on an empty stomach.

Another effort was made to disband the Mouse Patrol, as several students continued to allege that M.P. Leader *Gino Fuzzerelli* has been assigning all the best patrol routes to his close buddies. According to one source: "In the three weeks since they started the Patrol, those guys have blown up like blimps. This is a purrfect example of greed and corruption in student government."

Only one piece of business was actually concluded before the Council moved to adjourn to the refreshments table. By unanimouse vote, the Council went on
[Cont. p. 6, col. 2]

PAW PAW, Feb. 31—Tragedy struck Saint Paw High School Tuesday when top science student *Biff Nonsequitur* lost his ninth life to a trash compacter in his home. A member of Cat Scout Troop S-14, Biff was a winner of the Paw Paw 4S Achievement Award, and was building a mouse robot in his spare time.

"He must have been hungry or trying to figure out what that strange sound we kept hearing was," his friend *Bunsen Burns* said, "because he wandered out of the workshop and the next time I saw him he looked like a Rubik's Cube."

His previous lives were lost in incidents all related to his intense curiosity. If there is light, is there heat? (Fourth-degree burns in a house fire.) Is fur a good conductor? (Electrocution.) If you don't hold your breath when you swim underwater, will you drown? (Yes.)

A meowmorial service will be
[Cont. p. 3, col. 1]

DOG HIGH STUDENT COUNCIL SCANDAL CONTINUES

Feline Fashion
UP THE HALLWAYS DOWN THE CORRIDORS

Up the hallways down the corridors: with the new semester, an atmosphere of chic pervades Cat High. Here, some of our trendsetters model the latest in exciting new feline fashions.

For his cigarette break at Paw Paw Village Drug, **Jig Sawyer** favored the rough 'n' ready, casual chic of the Jordache sweatsuit. (He also favored it for dinner, for breakfast . . . and for the next six days.)

Stepping up to high fashion, **Trixie Nixon** wears an outfit from one of the hottest new designers: Norma Katmali. Behind her is **Canardly Telwat,** anticipating the spring season in naugahyde shorts and resortwear tennis shirt. In the background, Lars Endicatt (How about *taking* a few pix, Lars, instead of sneaking into them?)

More of the fun that's sweeping the Cat High set this season: **Cheryl Tigres** (right) is modeling one of the more whimsical pieces to be seen: the "postal stamp" shirt, an idea whose time may have come—but then again, maybe not. **T.S. Alleycat,** who always stands out in a crowd anyway, gains added presence in his Prince-of-Wales sweatpants and all-American, star-spangled sweater. The woolen cap, tipped rakishly over one eye, completes the effect. ("Fitzgerald wrote 'The Great Catsby' in one just like it," confides T.S.) **Sophie McMeow** completes the trio in a mouthwatering angora rabbit letter sweater, atop a sizzling silk moiré skirt. Way to go, Soph!

From his notoriously innovative and original wardrobe, **Harmon Cronin** has mished and mashed a bold graphic design (the Sylvester pullover) with pants in an upbeat plaid. Note the hat and sunglasses, which on any other cat might be *de trop* but on Harmon are the cat's whiskers. The seductively paw-printed arm belongs to Paloma Pawsano. (Her comment: "Where's the rest of me?")

The graceful posing of **Canardly Telwat** and **Sushi Chew** shows to great advantage two of this season's major trends: Canardly's white catsmere cardigan combines a softer, less "macho" fabric with the strong, masculine lines of the traditional tom's blazer. The polka-dot bow tie is another increasingly popular pattern, and is echoed in the pattern of Sushi's gently flaired skirt. Hey—did these two plan their outfits together this morning?

Christofurr F.E. Sandwich, ready as always to bowl the girls over, is sporting the **ne plus ultra** in acatdemic wear . . . simple, but nonetheless a statement of purrsonal style: the Cat High letter sweater. At left, **Kattja Wittagütz,** in a bold lemon-yellow chemise set off by sleek black leather (hmmm) accessories. In the background, one of our photographers, **Lars Endicatt.** "My camera is the only accessory I ever wear," says Lars.

Tiger O'Malley—sharp and suave in yet another version of the popular Cat High letter sweater—finds himself (lucky Tiger!) right smack in the middle of the skirt length controversy. At right, the lovely **Katta Wittagütz** in a clinging, knee-shrouding knit. At left, nubile junior Bonita Bliss, who, below her alluring "tropical" print blouse, flaunts a flouncy, daringly mid-thigh mini. Okay, Tiger, what's your preference? (Bet he takes both.)

THE LITTER

It was late into the storm—wraught September evening....The sky was a vacuous blue—black, the wind a callous crackling through the dying leaves of fall. I lay my ear to the sodden soil, and I listened.

The sound was faint, but unmistakable: the savage scratching of pencil-bearing paw against paper, the sound of creative cats in literary heat. It was happening! Closeted in Cheshire chambers, Cat High's Future Catulluses and Willa Catters were forging their odes, their wanton verbosities——perhaps the heartstrong tale of a lost chat chèri.

I rose slowly from the earth, contentedly stroked my lengthening whiskers, and even let escape an Angorran purr of delight. This was the genesis of The Litter, Volume 32, and I its editor. I turned for home, to partake of a pinch of Nicaraguan nip before turning in for the night.

T.S. Alleycat

"For C.F.E.S. III"

Oh, my soulmate,
Purrfect dreams we could nap together.
I think of you.
     Sometimes, under a fishbone sliver of moon,
With silken, quivering fur,
Dreaming in the sun,
I think of you.
     Proud tomcat,
As you stalk the halls,
I blush and draw back--into myself--
And I think of you.
     Myself, a she-cat who inside
Is a lioness,
No tame tabby, but a sleek jungle cat.
Do you think of me?
     Let us ride a catnip wave of wonder
Of whisker-tingling ecstasy,
Paw in paw in Paw Paw.
                    —Holly Mackerel

"Ode to a Goldfish"

Small and golden
the bowl
so open.
          E.Z.

Mouse, Mouse

Mouse, Mouse,
     I see you
     Scamper....
Into my hamper
Chase your little
     Face...
Chase your little
NOSE.
     Soon I grab
     You by the
toes.
     Does your stomach
     Turn at the sight
     Of moi?
     Are you tired of
     Running near and far?
     Too bad, too bad.
     This is your last week,
Because I'm going to catch your squeak, squeak, squeak!!!

T.S. Alleycat

Sample from the Reading Comprehension Section
of the CAT Test

From *A Tale of Two Kitties*, by Charles Chickens.

It was the best of times, it was the liverwurst of times; it was the age of smartycats, it was the age of fraidycats; it was the epoch of fresh tuna, it was the epoch of spilt milk; it was the season of Sylvester, it was the season of Tweety Bird; it was the premiere of "Cat on a Hot Tin Roof," it was a rerun of "The Meowly Tyler Moore Show"; it was the thrill of victory, it was the agony of defeat; we had everything going for us, but nothing was going right; we were all on our ninth trip to Pussy Heaven, we were all on our way to the tennis-string factory.

Questions

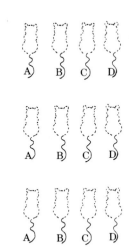

1. In this story, Tweety Bird is:
   (a) a whole lot better between two slices of rye.
   (b) jail bait.
   (c) an ugly duckling.
   (d) all of the above, not to mention a total dirtball.

2. What is Chickens trying to say about Pussy Heaven?
   (a) Nothing.
   (b) Home of the Whopper.
   (c) Not half bad, if you can afford the rent.
   (d) Great place for a bachelor party.

3. Choose the two words that best describe the tone of this story.
   (a) hanky, panky
   (b) hubba, hubba
   (c) pasteurized, homogenized
   (d) who, cares

Reading Comprehension II

It is July 27th. Spike, a bull mastiff, is sitting outside his dog house at 2:00 p.m. It is 95°. He is eating lunch, which consists of a bowl of dogfood. He is musing on the general composition of dogfood and its effects on the canine stomach. Suddenly, a black cat armed with a sub-machine gun and wearing a belt-full of grenades leaps over the fence and declares that he is hereby taking over the territory formerly known as Spike's Yard. Spike lets out a spine-chilling howl and charges toward the cat.

1. How long was it before Spike was discharged from the hospital?
   (a) 2 days
   (b) six weeks
   (c) 3 years, after serious complications and two severe bouts of
       indigestion during which he was in intensive care.
   (d) 4 hours—feet first.

2. In this story the feeling that all dogs are stupid is:
   (a) innuendo
   (b) implied
   (c) infurred
   (d) out of cat-text

3. The most appropriate title for this story would be:
   (a) "Dog Day Afternoon"
   (b) "Dog Eat Dog (food)"
   (c) "It's a Dog's Life"
   (d) "Doggone"

4. The black cat in the story is:
   (a) an antagonist
   (b) a protagonist
   (c) a podiatrist
   (d) trouble—with a capital T

Elementary Abstract Recognition Test

The EAR test is designed to test your elementary abstract recognition. Look at the figure in the box. You will notice that an important element is missing. Choose the element that will accurately complete the picture.

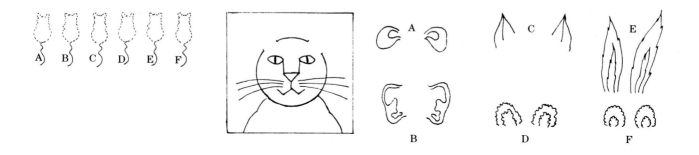

Sample Logic Questions

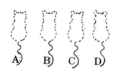

1. A cat can run 4 miles in one hour. A dog can run 6 miles in one hour. If a cat chases a dog for 2½ hours, what is the result?
   (a) Neither will be home for dinner.
   (b) The cat will ambush the dog at a fire hydrant on its way home.
   (c) Nothing. Would a cat ever run farther than from his recliner to the refrigerator?

2. Tongue:tuna; Brain:_____
   (a) Chopped Liver
   (b) Catnip
   (c) Napping
   (d) Fantasies

3. Tom Cat falls off the top of the World Trade Center, gets run over by the D train, bickers with a bulldog, slips while traversing a barbed wire fence, gets his head slammed in the refrigerator door, and falls off an ocean liner. How many lives does he have left?
   (a) 2
   (b) 4
   (c) 6
   (d) 8
   (e) Who do we appreciate?

4. Cat A, weighing 15 lbs., eats 10 lbs. of garbage for dinner. Cat B, weighing 10 lbs., eats 15 lbs. of garbage for dinner. Cat B pays for the meal. What does Cat A say?
   (a) No really, . . . let me . . .
   (b) O.K., next one's on me . . .
   (c) I'll leave the tip.
   (d) Burp . . . Yawn.

5. A house has ten lights. One light goes out. How many dogs does it take to screw in the light bulb?
   (a) 8. One to hold the ladder and seven to find a cat willing to consult.
   (b) 2. One to do it, and one to call the vet after the first one has been electrocuted.
   (c) You can't teach an old dog new tricks.
   (d) All of the above.

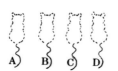

Abdul

—Photo by Tiger O'Malley.
Cindy Tab

How could anyone go through four (and in some cases five or six) years of Cat High and not be—er, uh—altered? From your first glimpse of **Principal Grimm** to your 101st double-take on his wife, life here has been one furreak-out after another.

The first time **Coach F. Ball Whiskers** ordered: "All right you *pussies!* Into the shower!" you were shocked by his alleycat manner. But the cold, fur-drenching waterfall that followed was the kind of catharsis that brought us freshkittens closer together!

Who would have thought this class needed sophomore sex lectures??? None of us could have guessed that Pokers-and-Dots (as we lovingly called it) could be so explicit? And how about the time **Mr. Humbert** went to the catatomical chart of the feline body and pulled down all of last year's Playcat centerfolds? Talk about revealing! And it was **Mike Redo**, as usual, who had done his damnedest to alter Cat High before Cat High altered him. What a stunning victory, even though it took him six years. And when we added it all up—who scored on who—it was: Redo 1,128, CH 2. (Two hold-backs for Mike, that is.)

It was in our junior year when, due to on-going caturity, many of our voices changed, and the Meowlers lost the last of their male sopurranos. What a thrill to be considered really adult on our first "Furmal" visit to Tux 'R' Us, to suit up for the prom. But along with the fun came responsibility:

With CATs and Driver's Ed we learned the values of both Stanley Katlan and fastening your seat belt when you take a driving lesson from Mr. Magoo…err, I mean **Culpepper**.

Things were changing so fast that by the time senior year rolled around we thought we'd seen it all. Were we ever wrong! Right on opening day this fall, **Claws McPaws**, no stranger to the Principal's office, picked a fight with **Eins** and **Zwei Katzenjammer**. "I bopped them with the ol' one-two," boasted Claws as the RATC patrol dragged him off to Principal Grimm's office, "and I don't like your *face*, you Chihuahua," he added, addressing Mr. Grimm, which pretty much summed up the way Claws felt about everybody all the time in his four years at Cat High. Claws was one of those cats who *never* changed.

But the rest of us went through enough changes to embarrass a chameleon, and about the biggest change for all of us in our four years at Cat High was getting used to the new cat in town this year. I saw him in my first bio class—this guy sitting there with a sheet on his head, looking like he's showed up two months early for Halloween. So for two weeks we all called him "UFO"—that's for Unidentified Foreign Oddball—but of course it was **Abdul Catdabra**, who turned out to be just about the coolest cat in a sheet you'd ever meet from Saudi Arabia.

The first Fish-on-Friday Feed was when Abdul showed us that you don't have to be

from Paw Paw to be purr-sonable. I mean, who can forget…First, the Anglers come up with the biggest salmon catch seen in Paw Paw since last year's toxic litter scare. Then **Oscar Hiss** puts on some Country Joe and the You-Know-What records he's just picked up at a close-out sale at Disco-Cat, and the next thing you know, there's Abdul, up on the table, inviting the whole class to visit his home town of Sandkatsle—all expenses paid!!!

A lot of us figured that the great change in going from junior to senior year would be that we'd get into R-rated movies. But except for "Animal House" (a true classic), the adult film fare was strictly for the birds: "Oh Catcutta!" was a cat-nap, and "Quest for Fur" (uggh) was a total gross-me-out. The PG action wasn't much to purr about either, with "Ordinary Cats" (featuring Meowly Tiger Moore) being just ordinary, and "Flash-prance" all wet. Only the Robert Redfurred retro-spective—"Barepaws in the Park," "Butch Catsidy and the Sundance Kitty," and "The Great Catsby"—really packed 'em in at the Fur Forum.

Of course, when you're talking changes, remember **Berkeley Fumes**'s ninth-grade nip party? That was probably our step through the looking glass.

A truly mind-expanding experience. (Berkeley gave new meaning to the expression "Cat High.") I'll never forget Mrs. Fumes coming home all hissterical and asking "Where's my little angel?"—and we all thought she was saying it just because of the little halos of smoke around Berk's ears. That's got to have been the wildest party in four years at Cat High. Of course, I heard that **Cindy Tab**'s pajama parties were pretty animalistic, but except for **Tiger O'Malley**, none of us guys ever got invited, so I couldn't say for sure.

Nobody—but nobody—changed like **Phyllis Snippit**. Actually, "Pinky" made a career of changing—changing her clothes, that is. You could always tell what the cat on the cover of *Cattymoiselle* was wearing—"Pinky" would be wearing it too. And who can forget the time she dyed her fur blond and announced, "If I have nine lives to live, let me live them as a blonde," to which **Berkeley Fumes** responded, "If I have nine lives to live, let me live them as a bong."

But then Phyllis wasn't the only cat in school who tried to keep up with the latest trends. It seemed that so many cats got their whiskers permed sophomore year that you could hardly tell the toms from the tabs. When punk-puss was in, so many Cat-Highers looked like dead ringers for **Spike Latigo** that even Spike got confused. And the Pritikitty Diet fad pulled in its share of devotees, but that didn't last

Culture comes to Paw Paw!

—thanks to Abdul's dad.

Lulu with the night's reading

Nick Sturgeon gives odds on who did it.

Looking for sympathy.

PAW PAW
VETERINARY
CLINIC

DUANE R. AKER DVM
HELEN B. ILL DVM

too long, since we all know there aren't too many cats who'd be caught dead eating raw vegetables.

One cat who did get caught dead was **Mike Redo**—on Senior Talent Night. Mike had 'em rolling in the aisles with his enactment of "101 Things To Do With A Dead Cat." Only **Wally Mackerel**, playing Carpo, **Ratsy Rizzo** (Nippo), and **Canardly Telwat** (Groucho) as the Manx Brothers wowed the crowd more than Mike.

Talent Night organizer **Stuart Ratatat** reported that ticket sales were solid enough to finance the entire class trip to Washington. Of course, most of the cats in the audience were our 'rents with their Polaroids and Insticatics. So when one of the parental pawpawrazzi called out to "watch the birdie," there was mass confusion in the auditorium, with everybody looking around and asking "Where? Where?"

Which was just the question the whole baseball team was asking when **Stanley Klinger**, breathless as usual, came running into the locker room and announced that **Ratsy Rizzo** was putting the moves on **Priscilla Pawsoff**. But by the time the team had found out where the action was taking place (it was in the chem lab), Prissy had busted Ratsy one in the chops, and cracked his shades, too, which made Ratsy *really* mad. This year things went a *little* more smoothly on the dating scene (thank God): As we all know, **Harmon Cronin** and **Sophie**

McMeow were the most harmonious thing this side of the Mormon Tabbynacle Choir, **Albert Cheshire** was hot and heavy with **Mira Nightingale**, and **Tiger O'Malley** was hot and heavy with just about everybody in skirts.

It seems obvious after four years of experience—and some got more than others—that relations between tabs and toms are not always clear sailing, as **Hobie Lufter** so succinctly put it. We can think of a couple of memorable non-romantic partnerships, however. Like the time **Curiosity Kildecat** (who could have believed our little Southern belle had it in her?) and **Mike Redo** (who else?) teamed up on their let's-all-flush-the-toilets-at-the-same-time-and-see-what-happens experiment. Now that prank brought on a flood of detentions and demerits, but who would deny that it was worth the hassle just to watch **Miss Maps** floating down the corridor. **Nick Sturgeon** was on top of the situation, as usual, giving great odds that she'd be carried at least as far as the baseball field. (She actually made it to third base—probably for the first time in her lives.)

Now that's the kind of team spirit that we've always shown as a class. If one of us has a great—or not so great—idea, the others will always pitch in to make sure the most possible chaos is created. Of course, sometimes we work together for educational gains, like during the class trip, when **Rufus Cubs** and the rest of the baseball team attempted to re-create George Washington's historical feat by throwing a dollar across the Potomac. They all agreed that Washington would've made one helluva center fielder if he'd really been able to do it, but then again, as Redo pointed out, a dollar went a helluva lot farther in those days.

Let's face it, Seniors, Cat High has taught us some invaluable lessons: accepting

Felicia Faye Tirebiter as one of our own...and learning never to call her a B%*!, right Prissy? ...appreciating the culture of our Africat roots in **Mr. Washington**'s study group (it was either that, or flunking the course)...and perhaps most important of all—learning that going "all the way" can litter up a cat's lives, but *good*. These and many other realizations will stay with us and bind us together, no matter how far we are from Cat High, or how sepurrated geographically. Whether we end up at Purrinceton, Ratgers, or Codfish Community College, our hearts and minds will always be in Paw Paw.

—Mark Mice
Editor-in-chief

GEORGE FRISKER

When the Yearbook Staff asked me to write this meowmorial for George, I wasn't sure I was the right cat for the job. Could I capture the essence of this top cat in a mere string of words? And besides, I never met George—not even once.

I heard a lot about him, though. It seems that everyone has vivid memories of George—especially the Cat High teachers, who had a special appreciation of George's classroom antics. That's because George would do almost anything for a laugh. And he usually got one, too—even if it meant a trip to Principal Grimm's office. Yes, George was living proof that charm isn't a four-letter word.

George had a love affair with life. I often heard of his beguiling smile, remembered by most Cat Highers as the "Frisker Whisker." The smile let him get away with just about anything—like cutting in line for seconds on milk at the Cateteria, and even stealing Alison Chow's answers on the CAT test. Sadly, though, George didn't get away with T-boning his beloved '67 Catalina on the front wall of Eddie's Shrimp and Bait Shop. Ironically, George was en route to the nine o'clock showing of "Dead Cats Don't Wear Plaid." He was wearing his plaid sharkskin suit.

So George is gone, but the lasting memories endure in the hearts of the cats who loved him: The Stray Cats jacket, the punk-puss 'do, the Mick Jaguar swagger, and the irrepressible Frisker Whisker. Adieu, George. The cats of Cat High will miss you.

Editor

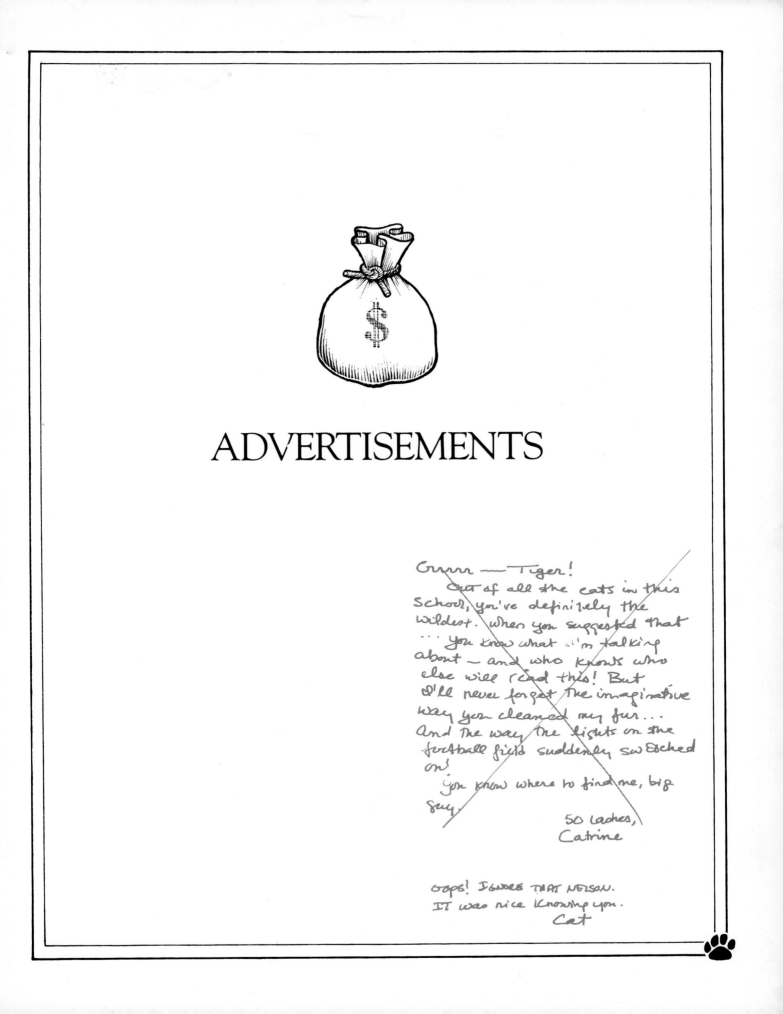

ADVERTISEMENTS

Grrrr — Tiger!
Out of all the cats in this
school, you've definitely the
wildest. When you suggested that
... you know what I'm talking
about — and who knows who
else will read this! But
I'll never forget the imaginative
way you cleaned my fur...
And the way the lights on the
football field suddenly switched
on!
You know where to find me, big
guy,
50 Lashes,
Catrine

Oops! Ignore that Nelson.
It was nice knowing you.
Cat

"Drugs are our only business"

Except for:

- Cosmetics
- Film
- Toys
- Malteds

- Ice Cream Sodas
- Sundaes
- Sundries
- Etc.

UNDER NEW MANAGEMENT

at PAW PAW and MAIN

RX1-1392

Baxter Loveset, the jerk behind the counter.

CATNIP MADNESS

CATNIP!

THE DEMON WEED!

- Catnip
- Nip
- The Nip
- K-nip
- Snip
- Snort
- Snarf
- Snoozing Powder
- Vitamin C
- Kit-Nap
- Napping Cure
- Experi-mint

All synonyms for one thing: Catnip, the demon drug
that has been plaguing society for centuries.

LEARN MORE ABOUT IT
BEFORE YOU TRY IT!!!

A Massage From the Editor

I would like to take this opportunity to thank all the individuals who contributed more than a lick and a promise to the creation of this year's *Paw Prints*. If it hadn't been for Miss Mouseberger's hectic schedule of time consuming non-yearbook duties and her appreciation of our lavish gifts, this could easily have been *just another yearbook*. Photography Editor Lars Endicatt and many of his she-cat assistants spent countless hours in the darkroom. They also developed and printed the images which grace these pages. And how could I forget to praise the Advertising Staff? Their efforts enabled several of us to miss a week of classes during the court trial. That'll teach us to misrepresent the demographics of Cat High!

I take great pride in this, the finished product, and do not regret for an instant the incredible amount of time I spent laboring over these pages—at times to the detriment of my school work. What remains is a lasting record of our years at Cat High. Some of you might disagree with the editorial tone. Remember—you didn't write it. Others may wonder why so many pictures of my friends were included. Did you buy me lunch nearly every day? But aside from any small quibbles you might have, you would be hard pressed to find fault with the over-all portrait of Cat High I have presented.

No cat is an island, and no book is without flaw. If you are having a problem with the binding, see Miss Mouseberger in room 222 for a partial refund. Bring your receipt.

Felicitations from,

Mark Mice
Editor-in-Chief

PAW PRINTS FINANCIAL STATEMENT

EXPENSES

Grooming for the co-editors	$ 55.45
Window shades	32.79
Plug for keyhole	.09
Typewriter for Business Manager (slightly bent)	8.00
Engravings, Printing	199.99
Covers	77.77
Travel and Entertainment for "Pussycats on Parade"	1385.98
Christmas gift for adviser Mouseberger	53.97
Thanksgiving gift for adviser Mouseberger	49.95
Court Fees for Advertising Manager	125.00
Loss from lending camera to Swim Team	179.99
Term papers for Darkroom Staff	90.00
Gold pen for Editor-in-Chief	438.89
Trophies for Miss Mouseberger	125.00
Bribe to Student Council for Adopting Budget	150.00
Total	**$3567.98**

INCOME

Received for flattering senior lines	$1233.53
Subscriptions from Student Body	87.99
Advertising (thanks to the Business Staff)	4.73
Received from Arbuckle for printing pictures	1200.00
Peeks at the yearbook dummy (Penny A Peek)	634.78
Income from "Pussycats on Parade"	.17
Long term loan from Abdul to balance budget	1422.04
Total	**$3567.98**

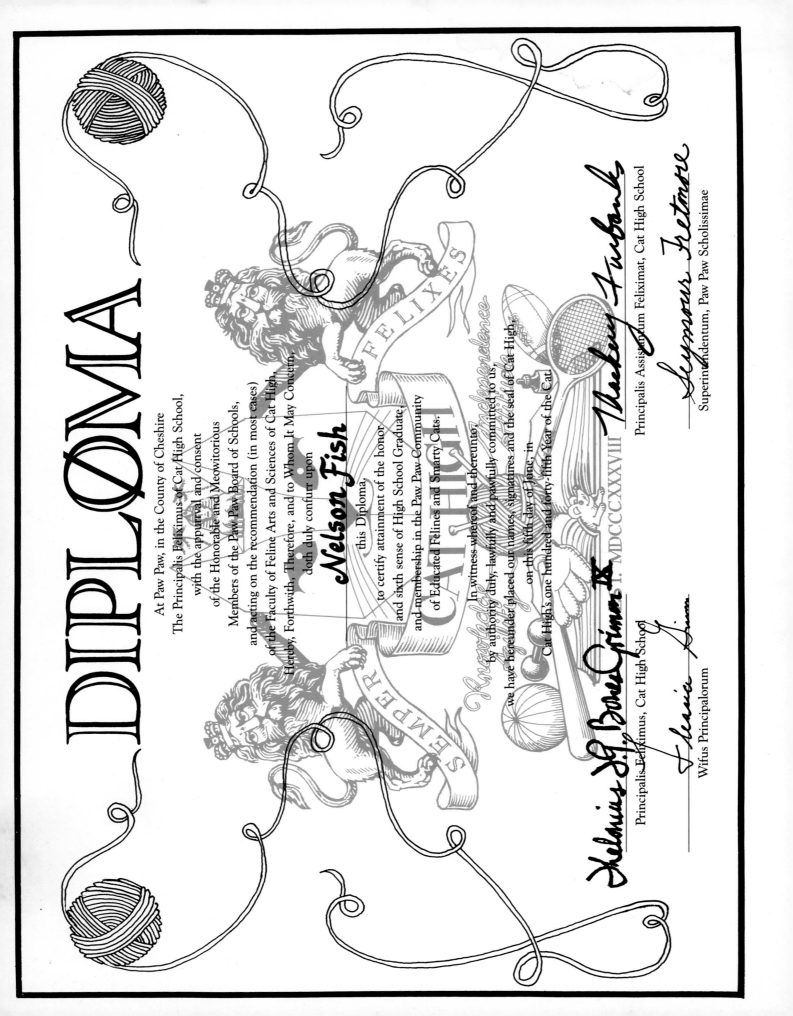

DIPLOMA

At Paw Paw, in the County of Cheshire

The Principalis Feliximus of Cat High School,
with the appurval and consent
of the Honorable and Meowitorious
Members of the Paw Paw Board of Schools,
and acting on the recommendation (in most cases)
of the Faculty of Feline Arts and Sciences of Cat High,
Hereby, Forthwith, Therefore, and to Whom It May Concern,
doth duly confur upon

Nelson Fish

this Diploma
to certify attainment of the honor
and sixth sense of High School Graduate,
and membership in the Paw Paw Community
of Educated Felines and Smarty Cats.

In witness whereof and thereunto
by authority duly, lawfully and pawfully committed to us,
we have hereunder placed our names, signatures and the seal of Cat High,
on this fifth day of June, in
Cat High's, one hundred and forty-fifth Year of the Cat

FELIXES

SEMPER

CAT HIGH I. MDCCCXXXVIII

Helvirus St. Bone Grimes IX
Principalis Feliximus, Cat High School

Flewie G.
Wifus Principalorum

Thackery Furbank
Principalis Assistorium Feliximat, Cat High School

Seymour Tretmore
Superintendentum, Paw Paw Scholissimae

Jay Brooks

Terry deRoy Gruber
Top Cat

"When you're done with that, I have something else for you to do."

AMBITION: To meet the deadline
LEAST LIKELY TO: Meet the deadline
WILL BE REMEMBERED FOR: His books
"Working Cats" (Harper & Row 1979) and
"Fat Cats" (Harper & Row 1981)
DONE FOR US LATELY: Created this book

Watch the birdie . . . try the other string
. . . maybe she'd like some baby food . . .
What should we do about dinner . . .

ACTIVITIES: Catnippers 1,2,3,4; Catbooks for a Better Society 4; Catnappers 2,3,4

I would like to thank the people whose talents, personalities, and school spirit united to create this book:
Polly Ellis, who started this project with me from scratch and got it soaring. Without Polly's sensitivity to cats, her patience, perseverance and managerial abilities *Cat High* could never have been erected.
Jay Brooks, who worked with me putting all the pieces together to finish the book. Were it not for Jay's imagination, artistic skills, and painstaking thoroughness the publisher would still be waiting for delivery.
Pat Carney, who came from Minneapolis to design the book, ended up "in detention" for an extra month while he refined our montage technique, wrote captions, in addition to doing the Carneyesque layouts and cover for *Cat High*. I would also like to thank my parents for their moral and financial support. My editor, Tom Congdon, for all the fine tuning he did on the copy and for the creative freedom he afforded me. And lastly, Elise O'Shaughnessy, thanks for the editing, writing, staff meals and overall perspective. And now scroll the credits:

• **Project Editor:** Tom Congdon • **Book and Cover Design:** Pat Carney • **Assistant Photographer/Editor:** Polly Ellis • **Assistant Editor/Photographer:** Jay Brooks • **Feature Writer:** Peter Oliver • **Staff Artist:** Pam Congdon • **Copy Editor:** Elise O'Shaughnessy • **Costume Design:** Susan Nickerson, Kathy Fredericks, Joan Clement, Lauren Brasco • **Additional Feature Writing:** Jack Laschever, Rich Hershlag, Elise O'Shaughnessy, Drew Moseley, Lisa Goren • **Special Props:** Alison Rewling • **Sets:** Louanne Gilleland • **Black and White Prints:** Mike Levins, Ken Gutmaker • **Special Graphics:** Michael Rowe • **Retouching:** Maritza Gutierrez, Rick Greco • **Backdrops:** Annette Sacks, Steve Adams • **Caricatures:** Dean Yeagle • **Additional Assistance:** Katherine Karr, Mary McCulley, Lisa Freeland, Ellen McManmon, Nancy Diamond, Lisa Portnuff, Irene Burtyk • **Additional Writing:** Jay Brooks, Pat Carney • **Additional Retouching:** Larry Risko, Jay Brooks, Vernon Allanby • **Additional Artwork:** Dave Rickerd, Elise O'Shaughnessy • **Yearbook Consultant:** Ron Weinman • **Typesetting:** Trufont Typographers • **Film Processing:** Portogallo Lab, Ken Gutmaker • **Book Printing:** Josten's American Yearbook Company • **Guardian Angel:** Michael Parman • **Special Material:** Julian de Rothschild Blau • **Late Nights at the Typewriter With:** Lisa Goren • **Chicken Fried Steak:** Tracey and Chris Marchbanks • **Xeroxing:** Penny Copy • **Thrift Store Guide:** Claire Acerno • **Sombreros from Mexico:** Mary and Bill Buell • **Special Thanks to:** Larry Ashmead, Joyce Wiggin at Eyes For the Needy, Cohen Optical, Alex Trento, Essex County Vocational School principal, Cathedral High School Vice Principal, George Lange, Garrett Loube, Cacky Sharpless, Sal and Star Taylor, The Hudson County Cat Club, Susan Patrizzi, the Catsino Cat Club, and Keestone Katz, Marianne Lawrence and the Black Jack Cat Club, Pam and Jim Swanson and the Chesapeake Cat Club, Mark Hanen and the CFA Southern Regional Cat Show, Bill Cummings and the Houston Cat Club, Empire Cat Club, C.F.A., T.I.C.A. • **Thanks for your help:** Jim Mullen, Artbar participants, Tony Sherer, Emily Greenspan, Jeff Wilmot, Wesley Strick, Anne Dayton, Lisa Claudy, Adam Feldman, Nick Goldberg, Marla Darling, Jamie deRoy, Michael Greer, Bert DePamphilis, Ariel Skelley, Gil Ortiz, Stephanie Klein, Margaret Goodenough, And thank you cats and cat owners:

• FACULTY AND ADMINISTRATION • **Mr. Bandersnatch:** B.J., Martie Fellman • **Miss Cordoba:** Barney, Kim Sloan • **Mr. Culpepper:** Khamen, Barbara Shearson • **Dr. Seymour Fretmore:** Bethlehem Steel, Esther Roppelt • **Thackery Furbanks:** Mittens, Dawn Reazs • **Fleasia Grimm:** Miss July Frost, Kathy Worthley • **Thelonius T.G. Bones Grimm IX:** Epi, Dave Mare • **Miss Hatch:** Lady Thoreau, Virginia Sullivan • **Mr. Humbert:** Azrael, Joe Watson • **Miss Maps:** Simon, Vikki Venne • **Mehitabel Mouseberger:** Daddy's Bandetti of Voo Doo, Pat and Gene Smith • **Mr. Nobull:** See Mr. Bandersnatch • **Mademoiselle Ouiounon:** Hope, Melinda Duncan • **Miss Parsely:** Summer, Carolyn Martin • **Mr. Ratterwrong:** Charpurr's Gigolo, Suzanne Stubblefield • **Miss Shugenah:** Moon Mighty, Roscoe Hough • SENIORS • **Alleycat,** T.S.: Sir Jasper of Ro Pa, Brenda and Richard Shelton • **Arbuckle,** Oedipuss: Panda, Marianne Lawrence • **Beads,** Rose: Mama Garfield, Steve and Leslie Russell • **Beelzebub,** Quentin: Purrkitz Princess Natasha Bonita, Jerome and Shirley Thomas • **Betterborn,** Chase Taylor: Ole Blue Eyes, Jo and Bill Cole • **Bootstraps,** Earnest: Mittens II, Tanya Gurreri • **Catdabra,** Abdul: Opal, Dina Villanvera • **Chatwick,** Catspurr: Perfect Surprise of Joyvyn, Joyce Pollina • **Cheshire,** Albert: Sparky, Dennis and Florence Lenaz • **Chew,** Sushi: Chit-chat Tara of Fen-Morrall, Mark Fensterstock • **Chow,** Alison: Tamara of Li Shou, Marsha Wadsworth • **Crawfish,** Joan: Gingham Girl, Ray and Marie Nowak • **Cronin,** Harmon: Tycoon, Judy Ries • **Cubs,** Rufus: Rufus, Virginia Sullivan • **Devereaux,** Collin: Rebel, Ron Hintz • **Dweezle,** Beasly: Maya Ariel Simba, Julia Reese • **Endicatt,** Lars: Rufus Raccoon, Anne Klutkowski • **Feleinberg,** Eva: Sunny, Samantha Brock • **Fish,** Nelson: Grand Champion Scottish Ears-2-Ya, Nancy Abbott and Gay Turner • **Fluffnutter,** Jane: Tiffany, Midge Michael • **Frisker,** George: Timochae, Carolyn Martin • **Fumes,** Berkeley: Calypso, Craig Brogand • **Fur,** Fred: Sir Rufus Velvetpaws, Karen Hauge • **Furlinghetti,** Zooey: Winston Churchill Proffitt, Cameron Lindsay Proffitt • **Fuzzerelli,** Eugene: Slugger, Ray and Marie Nowak • **Grouse,** Emma: Sugar Daddy, Vivian Painter • **Haddy,** Finn N: Toy, Valerie Weidel • **Hiss,** Oscar: Misha, Joan Connaghan • **Housecat,** Mary: Baby Kitty, Una Maderson • **Jones,** Ntgabwe: See Beezlebub, Quentin • **Katz,** Kitty Tyler: See Fur, Fred • **Katzenjammer,** Eins: Squeaky, Nancy Saxton • **Katzenjammer,** Zwei: Friskie, Nancy Saxton • **Khat,** Chaka: Inkspot, Mary Hare • **Kildecat,** Curiosity: Starship Tiffany, Cindy Popolillo • **Kitta,** Kunta: Scott, Louis W. Miller • **Klinger,** Stanley: Kallie, Lisa Freeland • **Knudsen,** Edsel: Queen Anne's Lace, Lori Entwistle • **Latigo,** Spike: Shotoku Bronwen of Shikotan, Barbara Carlough • **Lick,** Melvin: Jesse Joe Cat, Danielle and Mellina Murray • **Liverston,** Stanley: Special, Katrina J. Williams • **Lovecat,** Sunshine: Race Citty, Diane C. Schierle • **Loveset,** Baxter: Grand Premier Aldebaran's Galileo, Linda Jones • **Lufter,** Hobart: Charlie Lucky Luccianno, Danielle and Mellina Murray • **Mackerel,** Holly: Scottish Impossible Miracle, Nancy Abbott • **Mackerel,** Wally: See Mackerel, Holly • **MacLeash,** Clawford: Laplumes Plaid Dodi, Newton West • **Madison,** Pawline: Kitty, Sam Del Propost • **Mange,** Allen: Piglet, Michele and Toni Rogers • **McMeow,** Sophie: Dahlia, Cindy Popolillo • **McPaws,** Claws: Fatso, Denise Bull • **McWhiskers,** Millicent: Chelsea, Camille Horan • **Messeroffski,** Chip: Barry Lyndon, Ilda Zukowski • **Mice,** Mark: Talese, Terry Gruber • **Mousehaus,** Annemarie: E.T., Anita Rossien • **Nightingale,** Mira: Mira, Candy Schaffes • **Nixon,** Trixie: Shikotan Cattery Weebles, Barbara Carlough • **Nosely,** Agatha: See Alleycat, T.S., Brenda and Richard Shelton • **O'Malley,** Tiger: Lil' Red #2, Joyce Nankervis • **O'Ninetails,** Catrine: See Fish, Nelson • **Pawsano,** Paloma: Marmelade, Conrad and Phyllis Milster • **Pawsoff,** Priscilla: Angel, Michele and Tony Rogers • **Purr,** Sue: Rockport Red, Lesley Russell • **Quasar,** Kirk: T.J., Pat Glass • **Ratatat,** Stuart: Khamen, Barbara Shearson • **Redo,** Mike: Bo, Victoria Loftin • **Rizzo,** Ratsy: Sunsplash, Kathy Worthley • **Sandwich,** Christofurr Fenwick Eggenliver III: Fred the Furrier, Linda and Michelle Fernandez • **Sawyer,** Jig: See Knudsen, Edsel • **Smelts,** Edna: Tortie, Tracey Davidson • **Snippitt,** Phylliss: Ish, Helen Watson • **Squeeks,** Waylon: Kisacats Solomon's Seal of De-Miara • **Sturgeon,** Nick: Spanky, Louis W. Miller • **Tab,** Cindy: Demetrius Too, Ginny Nugent • **Telwat,** Canardly: Penelope, Mark Fensterstock • **Tigres,** Cheryl: Guantanamo II, Ray and Marie Nowak • **Tirebiter,** Felicia Faye: Henry, Tracy Broderick • **Tumi,** Saki: Patchwork, Joan Foster • **Twitchfit,** Lulu: Ch. Longbrook's Crystal Cryssie, Jean B. Townsend • **Van Purr Purr,** Pawpurr: See Mange, Allen • **Von Furstenbreed,** Felicity: Little Romeo, Margit Green • **Winchester,** Chester: Torvmyra's Gershwin of Royal Hylands, Ted and Susan Margwarth • **Witdagutz,** Kattja: Teddy Bear, Kathryn Martin • **Yikes,** Teresa: Popoki Or Chaiya, Carole Gradick • **Yung,** Yin and Yang: Glissade and Feats, Lynn Von Egidy • **Zooaster,** Ezekiel: See McPaws, Claws • **Zoose,** Pyewacket: Cassie, Thomas and Mary Martin • JUNIORS • **Bliss,** Bonita: Lucy, Virginia Sullivan • **Dactyl,** Polly: See Fleasia Grimm • **Jalapiña,** José: Moon, Drew Moseley • **Johnson,** Stretch: Abba Dabba Doo, Jim and Donna Cooper • **Lyons,** Louise: Puffalong Cassidy, Linda and Michele Fernandez • MUSICIAN • **Rastafurr:** Tenchy, Minamarie Day • CATS IN HATS • **Chef Le Pan:** Mao Tse-Tung aka Mousie, Jay Brooks • **Leo Lukashewski:** Trumpkin, the Congdons • **Vinnie Ishkibble:** Nina, the Congdons • **Mr. Joe Joe:** See Catdabra, Abdul • SUPPORT STAFF • **Nurse Hummingbird:** See Fleasia Grimm • **F. Ball Whiskers:** Lucky, Sue Birn • **Mrs. Withers:** Sprinkle, Denise Shaffer

PAWTOGRAPHS